An Introduction to
DIGITAL IMAGE PROCESSING

WAYNE NIBLACK

Prentice/Hall PHI International

Englewood Cliffs, New Jersey   London   Mexico   New Delhi
Rio de Janeiro   Singapore   Sydney   Tokyo   Toronto   Wellington

---
Library of Congress Cataloging in Publication Data

Niblack, Wayne
  An introduction to digital image processing.

  Bibliography: p.
  Includes index. 1. Image processing — digital techniques.
  I. Title. TA1632.N53 1986 621.36'7 86-5093

  ISBN 0-13-480674-3

British Library Cataloguing in Publication Data

Niblack, Wayne
  An introduction to digital image processing.
  1. Image processing — Digital techniques
  I Title
  621.38'0414   TA1632

  ISBN 0-13-480674-3

First published 1985 by Strandberg Publishing Company.
3460 Birkeroed, Denmark
This edition © 1986 Prentice-Hall International (UK) Ltd

Prentice-Hall, Inc., *Englewood Cliffs, New Jersey*
Prentice-Hall International (UK) Ltd, *London*
Prentice-Hall of Australia Pty Ltd, *Sydney*
Prentice-Hall Canada Inc., *Toronto*
Prentice-Hall Hispanoamericana S.A., *Mexico*
Prentice-Hall of India Private Ltd, *New Delhi*
Prentice-Hall of Japan Inc., *Tokyo*
Prentice-Hall of Southeast Asia Pte Ltd, *Singapore*
Editora Prentice-Hall do Brasil Ltda, *Rio de Janeiro*
Whitehall Books Ltd, *Wellington, New Zealand*

Printed and bound in Denmark for
Prentice-Hall International (UK) Ltd,
66 Wood Lane End, Hemel Hempstead, Hertfordshire, HP2 4RG
by Strandberg Bogtryk/Offset a.s., 3460 Birkeroed

1 2 3 4 5   90 89 88 87 86

ISBN 0-13-480674-3

Preface

Digital image processing is a fascinating and challenging field. It is fascinating because of the possibilities it offers, and it is challenging because, in the final analysis, it is often trying to "understand" and "improve" a digital image, which is just a large array of numbers, and this has proved to be no simple task. In addition, digital image processing is a rapidly growing field. This is due, at least in part, to recent advances in desktop and personal computers. Useful functions can now be performed in relatively small and inexpensive computer systems in offices, labs, and manufacturing locations.

This book covers many of the fundamental operations that are used in digital image processing. What it covers may be called two-dimensional, multi-valued digital image processing. It is intended for use in a university level course in which the students have had calculus, vector algebra, elementary statistics, and preferably some exposure to the Fourier transform. Its subject matter is the methods and applications of digital image processing, as opposed to the underlying hardware. The book grew from a set of notes I prepared while giving such a course at the Technical University of Denmark during a one year sabbatical leave from IBM.

There are several unique features to this book, and I mention two of them. First, it is intended as a textbook, not a reference book. The material can be covered in a one semester course, including time for "hands on" sessions and programming projects, and problems have been included in each chapter to get the student involved in the material. Secondly, it contains a large chapter on image display. This operation, which is used in all image processing systems, is covered only briefly in many other books, and a growing number of methods are now available to achieve informative and pleasing displays.

Programming considerations are rarely mentioned in the book although they are an important part of a course in digital image processing. As part of the course for which this book was prepared, students wrote programs and applied them to images. Some of the programs were fairly large, requiring over 1000 lines of high level, usually PASCAL, code. These programming projects were an extremely valuable part of the course, and are recommended for any similar course. There is nothing like programming an algorithm to ensure a thorough understanding of it, and the actual versus anticipated results give a student (or anyone else) an appreciation for some of the difficulties in digital image processing.

Wayne Niblack

Acknowledgements

During the preparation of this book, I received excellent help from many individuals. Some of this help was in the form of administrative and logistical support, and, in this category, I wish first to thank Professor Preben Gudmandsen of the Electromagnetics Institute (EMI), Technical University of Denmark not only for arranging my one-year position as a guest professor there but also for allowing me, during much of that year, to concentrate on the preparation of the course and course material from which this book grew. I also warmly thank Johan Teglhøj of IBM Denmark for his constant and many-faceted support, and Lis Bergqvist, also of IBM Denmark, who patiently drew the figures and prepared the manuscript for printing. The excellent photographic work of Lasse Rusborg, EMI, is acknowledged, as is the cooperation and support of Hans Jørgen Strandberg, the publisher.

A second category of help was technical. Leif Toudal Pedersen and Preben Hansen, both of EMI, and Kjeld Rasmussen of the Geographical Institute, Copenhagen University, each reviewed portions of the manuscript and their corrections and helpful suggestions are gratefully acknowledged. Preben also provided results for Figure 53 and Figure 54, and Leif provided software routines to help generate Figure 24. I received much help from my colleagues working in digital image processing in the IBM Scientific and Research Centers. From the center in Paris, I thank Louis Asfar, from whose work some of the material in Chapter 5 is adopted, Mario Hernandez, who provided programming support for some of the examples of Chapter 7, and P. T. Nguyen. I also thank other members of the Center with whom I worked on the development of the High Level Image Processing System (HLIPS), the software system used to generate many of the color and black-and-white images in the figures, and Rene Moreau, who was director of the center, for supporting my work while I was there. From the UK Center, I thank Rhys Lewis for his excellent suggestions as well as for Figure 48 and Figure 49 (generated using the IAX image processing system), Mike Cocklin, who provided Figure 21 and Figure 45 (also generated using IAX), Mike Cowlishaw, Dave Stevenson, and Steve Davies. Antonio Santestiban and M. Narciso of the Madrid Center were helpful, and from the same center, I particularly thank Francisco Ramirez. Figure 35 and Figure 62 are but two examples of many figures generated using software routines he developed for HLIPS. Mike Felix, IBM Graphic System Programs, was helpful in several ways, providing test images and utility programs, and Ed Farrell, IBM Yorktown, kindly provided Figure 33(d). Birger Niss of the NEUCC, the regional computing center located at the Technical University of Denmark, provided the data of NGC 1851, the astronomy image used in text, as well as frequent support in using the NEUCC computing facilities. Finally in the category of technical help, I would like to thank my students. They endured both my lectures and the early versions of portions of this book. In addition, many of them did excellent work on the projects they were assigned as part of the course, and some of their work has been included in this book. These include the results of Jan Madsen and Per Berg (Figure 86), Jørgen Fabrin and Benny Jensen (Figure 27), Nis Engholm and Christian Saxtoft (Figure 51), Klaus Gram-Hansen and Jens Christian Lauritzen (Figure 61), Allan Petersen and Ole Tidemann (Figure 34), and a modified form of the results of Peter Raaby and Jan Petersen (Figure 56).

A final category of help is simply support and encouragement. For this, I would like to thank above all my wife Janet, who kept our family running smoothly and cheerfully while I became engrossed in the preparation of this book.

To
Sam, Laura, David, Vicky,
and Janet

Contents

1.0 Getting Started

1.1 Introduction

Digital image processing has been used to determine the brightness of stars in a picture from a telescope, to determine the structure of a virus in a microscope image, and to produce highly accurate maps of the earth from satellite-gathered pictures. It has been used to control a sausage slicing machine to get equal weight slices from the irregularly shaped sausage, to design textile patterns prior to weaving, and to help restore classic paintings. It has applications in medicine, cartography, industry, manufacturing, printing and publishing, cosmetics and personal grooming, and a host of scientific and research fields including astronomy, mineral analysis, fluid mechanics, radioactive analysis, particle physics, and ocean modelling.

In all cases, digital image processing is concerned with the computer processing of pictures or, more generally, images that have been converted into a numeric form. These images come from many sources. Cameras, called digital cameras, are available that produce digital images instead of the classic piece of exposed film, and any photograph can be digitized by using devices called scanners or microdensitometers. In fields such as medicine, materials testing, and astronomy, instruments are available that produce digital images from X-rays, gamma rays, and ultrasound waves. Satellite sensors directly produce digital images from measurements of reflected or emitted visible, infrared, or microwave radiation.

In general, the purpose of digital image processing is to enhance or improve the image in some way, or to extract information from it. Typical operations are to:
  - Remove the blur from an image
  - Smooth out the graininess, speckle, or noise in an image

- Improve the contrast or other visual properties of an image prior to displaying it
- Segment an image into regions such as object and background
- Magnify, minify, or rotate an image
- Remove warps or distortions from an image
- Code the image in some efficient way for storage or transmission

Many of these operations are described in this book.

For a new reader, the questions may arise "Why the 'digital' in digital image processing? Are there others kinds of image processing and what is special about the digital kind?" Yes, there are other kinds, mainly (1) optical and photographic, and (2) electrical analog. The first includes the use of lenses, enlargers, and the many photographic techniques such as dodging and unsharp masking to scale, vary colors, reduce blur and so on in pictures. The second kind covers standard television in which images are converted into electrical signals (but not numbers as in digital image processing), transmitted, received, and reconstructed as pictures. Both of these fields are capable of complex operations. However, digital image processing offers two main advantages. The first is precision. In each generation of photographic process, there is a loss of image quality, and electrical signals are degraded by the physical limitations of the electrical components, whereas digital image processing can essentially maintain exact precision. The second advantage is its extreme flexibility. Using an enlarger, an image may be magnified, but in digital image processing, one part may be magnified, another reduced, another rotated, and so on. The contrast and brightness of a television picture may be adjusted, but in digital image processing, literally dozens of adjustments can be made. The contrast and brightness may be adjusted, the adjustment may be irregular, it may be discontinuous, it may be limited to some part of the image or varied throughout the image, and on and on. The main disadvantages of digital processing are its speed and expense. Many of its operations are slower than the corresponding optical or electrical operations, and the computing resources may be expensive. But these factors have been greatly reduced by the recent advances in comput-

	Output	
	Image	Description
Input Image	Image Processing	Image Pattern Recognition, Computer Vision
Input Description	Computer Graphics	Other Data Processing

Figure 1. Fields related to the computer processing of images.

er technology and the associated lower cost. Many useful digital image processing operations are now available on personal computers and desktop workstations. In fact, several of the example operations mentioned in the opening paragraph have been implemented on such systems.

Other fields also deal with the computer processing of images, and Figure 1 shows one way of categorizing them: by the type of input they take and the type of results or outputs they produce. Image processing typically takes an image as input and produces an image as output, where the output image is enhanced or corrected in some way. Computer graphics is concerned with producing images as output, but the input is descriptive information. Examples of the output images are line drawings for engineering use or three dimensional views of an object with effects for shading, lighting, surface material, observer position, and so forth. The descriptive input information could be words like "chair" or "table", but at a lower level is detailed information such as object dimensions, shape, color, and reflecting properties, say dull or shiny. Image pattern recognition takes an image as input and produces descriptive information as output. This is, in some sense, the reverse of computer graphics. An example is a count of the number and type of cells in an image from microbiology. Or it may produce the shape and color descriptors

40	40	40	40	40	40	40	40	40	40	40
40	40	40	40	200	200	200	40	40	40	40
40	40	40	40	200	200	200	40	40	40	40
40	40	40	40	200	200	200	40	40	40	40
40	200	200	200	200	200	200	200	200	200	40
40	200	200	200	200	200	200	200	200	200	40
40	200	200	200	200	200	200	200	200	200	40
40	40	40	40	200	200	200	40	40	40	40
40	40	40	40	200	200	200	40	40	40	40
40	40	40	40	200	200	200	40	40	40	40
40	40	40	40	40	40	40	40	40	40	40

Figure 2. A simple digital image: (a) The image and (b) the corresponding array of numbers.

used by computer graphics. Still another field, computer vision, includes many topics from image processing and image pattern recognition, but is broader in the sense that it is concerned with a complete system, a "seeing machine". Problems typical of computer vision include image acquisition (how many cameras are needed? where should they be placed?), motion (tracking objects as they move), and three dimensional aspects (what is the three dimensional shape and position of an object, or of the camera itself, which may be mounted on a movable robot arm?).

In this book, we will be concerned only with image processing: taking in an image, processing it, and outputting another image.

1.2 Some Basic Concepts

Image, Pixels, and Bands. An image is a picture, photograph, display, or other form giving a visual representation of an object or scene. However, in digital image processing, it has another meaning: an image is a two dimensional array of numbers. Figure 2 (a) is an image of a simple geometric pattern, and part (b) is the corresponding digital image. The digital image has eleven lines and eleven samples per line. Each number in (b) corresponds to one small area of the visual image, and the number gives the level of darkness or lightness of the area. We will assume that the higher the number, the lighter the area, so zero is black, the maximum value is white, and intermediate values are shades of grey. (This is arbitrary and could be done the other way around---zero equal to white, and so on.) Each small area to which a number is assigned is called a "pixel", which is short for picture element. The size of the physical area represented by a pixel is called the spatial resolution of the pixel. This varies greatly, from a few nanometers in microscope images to tens of kilometers in satellite images. Each pixel has its value, plus a line coordinate and a sample coordinate. These give its location in the image array. For example, the pixel at line 3, sample 2 (which has the box around it) has value 40.

We will always assume that images are rectangular arrays; that is, there are nl lines in the image, and ns samples in each line. Often images are square, and typical image sizes are 256 x 256, 512 x 512, and 1024 x 1024.

The minimum value a pixel can have is typically 0, and the maximum depends on how the number is stored in the computer. Different formats allow different maximums. One way is to store each pixel as a single bit, which means it can take only the values 0 and 1, or black and white. Another common way is to store each pixel as a byte, which is 8 bits. In this form the maximum pixel value is 255. Other formats are possible, and vary somewhat depending on the computer architecture. Examples are halfword integer, 16 bits per pixel, or floating point, usually 32 bits per pixel. These allow greater precision and range of pixel values, but require, respectively, two and four times as much computer memory to store the image. Because images are often large to begin with, these formats are less often used. In byte format, pixel values can only be integers, and not, for example, 4.25 or other fractional numbers. Integers are sufficient for most purposes, and byte format is the form we will normally use. When calculations are performed on the pixel values that require fractional precision, a final step of rounding or truncation is assumed.

13	14	14	14	14	15	13	13	13
14	13	14	14	13	14	14	13	14
14	15	15	19	21	14	15	13	12
17	26	34	37	39	21	14	16	15
36	32	27	27	36	21	13	14	14
28	34	34	27	34	19	14	14	14
31	38	32	35	34	18	15	14	13
27	34	28	39	36	15	15	15	15
30	32	27	40	33	17	15	14	15

Figure 3. : A digital image taken from satellite. Pixel values from the area in the box are shown.

When displaying a digital image, for example on a cathode ray tube (CRT), that is, a TV type device, or as a picture on a piece of film, each pixel controls the brightness level of one small spot. A typical spot size is 1/4 mm, or about 0.01 inch, for CRT displays, and may be smaller on printing devices. At these scales, the blockiness of the image is not normally noticeable. In this respect, the image of Figure 2 is not typical; each pixel is displayed as a spot on the page of about 4 mm. Figure 3 is more normal. It shows part of a digital image taken by a satellite mounted sensor, and is displayed with pixels at about 1/4 mm. The blockiness is not noticeable. A small portion of the pixel values is shown. For this image, the spatial resolution of the pixels is 30 m^2.

A scene may have several images associated with it. For example, when dealing with color, we may have images of the three components red, green, and blue. Multispectral scanner instruments flown on aircraft and satellites typically gather from 3 to 11 images. Figure 4 illustrates such a case. All images are collectively referred to as "the image", the individual images as "bands" of the image, and we may speak, for example, of the red band of an image. In most cases, the bands are considered to be aligned so that they su-

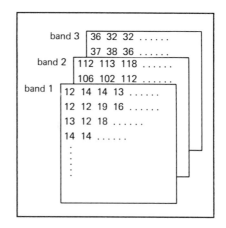

Figure 4. A three band image.

perimpose and can, for example, be displayed on the three colors of a color display monitor with no shift or displacement between them.

The Image Histogram. Often we would like to have some measure of the distribution of the pixel values in an image. We can use the mean $\bar{v}$ and standard deviation σ:

$$\bar{v} = \frac{1}{n}\sum_{i,j} v(i,j) \qquad \sigma = \sqrt{\frac{1}{n}\sum_{i,j} \left(v(i,j) - \bar{v}\right)^2}$$

where n is the number of pixels in the image. In addition to these, one of the most common measures of the pixel values in a (single band) image is a table giving the number of pixels having each possible value v. This table, which is often given as a plot, is called the image histogram and we denote it by $h(v)$. An example is shown in Figure 5. The domain of the histogram is the set of possible pixel values. If the image has 8 bit pixels, this is the interval 0 to 255. The histogram may be computed over the entire image, or only over a portion of the image which is of interest. If n_a is the number of pixels in the area over which the histogram is computed, it is easy to see that:

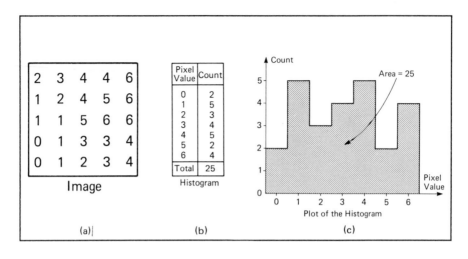

Figure 5. The one dimensional histogram: The histogram of the image in (a) may be represented as a table (b) or as a plot (c).

$$\sum_v h(v) = n_a$$

Often the histogram is normalized:

$$H(v) = \frac{h(v)}{n_a}$$

$H(v)$ is analogous to the probability density function of statistics, and may be considered as the probablility of a pixel having value v. In this case,

$$\sum_v H(v) = 1$$

For two bands and a specified area, we may also compute a two dimensional table $h(v,w)$ giving the number of pixels having value v in the first band and value w in the second. This is called the two dimensional histogram, or sometimes the scatterplot or scatterdia-

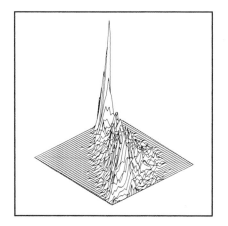

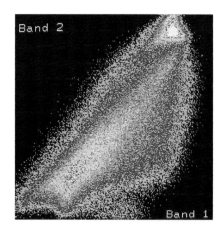

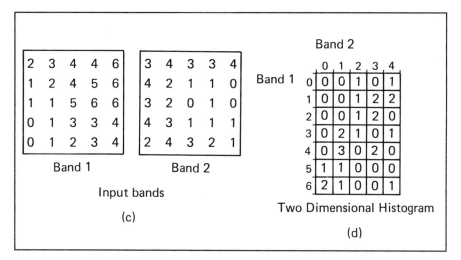

Band 1
Band 1 \ Band 2	0	1	2	3	4
0	0	0	1	0	1
1	0	0	1	2	2
2	0	0	1	2	0
3	0	2	1	0	1
4	0	3	0	2	0
5	1	1	0	0	0
6	2	1	0	0	1

Two Dimensional Histogram

(d)

Input bands

(c)

Figure 6. The two dimensional histogram $h(v,w)$: In (a), the plot is shown in perspective with $h(v,w)$ the height at point (v,w), and in (b), $h(v,w)$ is given by the color in the two dimensional v-w plane. For the example bands shown in (c), the 2d histogram is given in (d).

gram, of the two bands. Examples are shown in Figure 6. The domain of $h(v,w)$ is the rectangular region of the plane bounded by $(0, v_{max})$ and $(0, w_{max})$. For 8 bit pixels, this is the region (0,255) x (0,255). Similar to the one dimensional histogram, the two dimensional histogram satisfies:

$$\sum_{v} \sum_{w} h(v,w) = n_a$$

for n_a the number of pixels in the area of the histogram.

2.0   Image Display

One of the fundamental operations of digital image processing is that of displaying images. They may be displayed on CRTs, or on hard copy devices such as printers and photographic equipment. The images may be displayed as monochromatic (a single color, such as green), achromatic (shades of grey, often called "black and white"), or in color. For our purposes, monochromatic and achromatic are equivalent.

When displaying an image on a CRT, the intensity at each point on the screen is controlled by the value of the corresponding pixel in the image. A monochrome CRT has one component, say lightness-darkness, that may be controlled for each point. A color CRT has three components at each point, red, green, and blue. Each component is independently controlled and we speak of applying a band of an image to the "red gun", one to the "blue gun", and one to the "green gun". Typical problems in displaying an image are:

1. For a monochromatic display, how should the image control the display? That is, how should each pixel value control the intensity at the corresponding point---linearly, logarithmically, etc.--- to produce a pleasing display and show the detail in the image?
2. For a color display of three bands, how should the bands be assigned to the color components? The simplest solution is to let each gun be controlled by one band, but there are other possibilities. And similar to the monochromatic displays, how does each band control each gun?
3. For a color display, what if we only have one or two bands? Or more than three?

The solution to these problems depends on the nature of the data, the particular features of interest in the image, and so on. In addition, it depends on properties of the observer, which is presumably a human. Therefore we begin by looking at some properties of the human visual system and some topics from color science, and then go into methods for displaying images.

2.1 Some Topics from Human Vision and Color Science

The Human Visual System and Tristimulus Color Theory

The Bible says that we are "fearfully and wonderfully made." This is certainly evident for the human visual system, which includes the eye, the optic nerve, and parts of the brain. This system is highly adaptive and non-uniform in many respects, and by recognizing and compensating for these non-uniformities we can produce improved displays for many images. Some of its properties are physiological, depending on physical characteristics of the human eye, and others are psychophysical, depending on both the characteristics of the eye and the brain. Quantitative measurements are difficult, and much of the experimental data is subjective. Standards for many of these have been set by the Commission Internationale d'Eclairage (CIE), an international organization concerned with measurements of light and color.

We list here some of these standards, some related experimental results regarding human perception of color and brightness, and describe some basic elements of tristimulus color theory.

Brightness Perception as a Function of Wavelength. The curve $V(\lambda)$ in Figure 7(a) is called the Relative Luminous Efficiency Function or the Relative Luminosity Function. It gives the relative brightness of light of a constant energy and a single wavelength as a function of the wavelength as perceived by a "standard observer". It is essentially the response function, or spectral sensitivity, of the human eye. The eye is adaptive to the surrounding light level, and what is plotted in the figure is applicable for normal daytime light levels when "photopic" vision is dominant. The curve is also called the Photopic

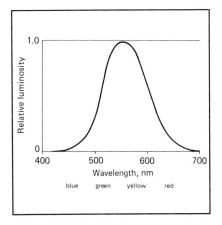

Figure 7. Human perception of brightness: (a) The Relative Luminosity Function V(λ) (Photopic) showing brightness perception as a function of wavelength. (b) Examples of the subjective nature of brightness perception. Top: Near the actual brightness steps, you see apparent bands of lightness or darkness called Mach bands. Bottom: The two center boxes are the same brightness, but the one on the darker background appears brighter. This effect is called simultaneous contrast.

Luminosity Function. A similar curve, the Scotopic Luminostiy Function, is applicable for low light levels, corresponding to "night vision", but the Photopic Luminosity Function is the one applicable for displays used in digital image processing. The function shows that the eye is most sensitive to brightness in the yellow-green. For example, a light radiating a fixed amount of energy in yellow will appear brighter to an observer than a light radiating the same amount of energy in blue. This has implications in digital image processing, for example, in case a multi-colored but uniform brightness display is desired.

Definition of Luminance of a Color or Light Source. The Relative Luminosity Function $V(\lambda)$ provides a way of defining the brightness or luminance of a light source of a single wavelength, but it may also be extended to define the luminance of an arbitrary light source. Viewing angle and geometry also affect brightness, but we will assume these are fixed, in which case the luminance of a color with spectral energy distribution $c(\lambda)$, that is, time rate of energy emitted per unit wavelength, is given by:

$$L = k \int c(\lambda) \, V(\lambda) \, d\lambda$$

where k is a scaling constant. In this definition, we must remember that a fixed viewing angle and distance are assumed.

The terms brightness and luminance have been used almost synonymously above. However there is a difference. Brightness refers to the subjective quantity describing how an observer sees a light. Luminance, as defined above, is a psychophysical, measurable property of the light. The two are related, and in normal viewing conditions they are directly related. But in some cases a light of a lower luminance appears brighter. Figure 7(b) shows two examples: Mach bands, perceived bands of a different brightness near a border of actual brightness change, and simultaneous contrast, the difference in perceived brightness of an area as a function of background brightness. A third term that is also used is intensity, often for the idea of brightness. Of the three, only luminance has a precise definition. The others, particularly intensity, have no fixed definitions and are used loosely or defined in a particular way for a specific application.

Some Elements of Tristimulus Color Theory. From mixing paints as a child, everyone knows that colors can be mixed together to produce new colors. Also, many people realize that a color television uses only three color guns, red, green, and blue, to produce its pictures. These pictures have a wide range of colors and are made by mixing the red, green, and blue. Many of the properties of color mixing and of human perception of color are explained by tristimulus color theory. One of the theory's basic tenets is that a color, as perceived by a human, can be expressed as a triplet of numbers (r,g,b). This is somewhat surprizing if we think of light as electromagnetic radiation, in which case it would seem that a continuous curve over the visible spectrum (about 380 to 750 nanometers), would be required. However, because of the mixing, only three "primaries" R, G, and B are needed, and any other color C can be mixed from the primaries. The triplet (r,g,b) gives the amount of the primaries R, G, and B that must be mixed to produce C:

$$C = rR + gG + bB$$

Equal here means perceived as the same color by an observer. We have used R, G, and B, suggesting primaries of red, green, and blue, but it turns out that any three colors may be used as primaries as long as they are independent; that is, no one of them can be mixed from the other two.

Many color matching experiments have been performed using various sets of primaries. Either an input color can be matched directly as a mixture of the three, or one or two of the primaries must be added to the given color and then this can be matched with the remaining primaries. In this case, the coefficients of the added primaries are considered negative. However, the point is that, by including negative coefficients, any color can be matched with any three independent primaries. It is the case that any set of physical primaries will need some negative coefficients to match some colors. Certain shades of red, green, and blue give the broadest range of mixable colors for positive coefficients. Thus they are used, for example, in color television since a physical device cannot produce negative amounts of a primary.[1]

To avoid negative coefficients, the CIE defined, as an international standard, a set of non-physical primaries that allows any color to be specified by a triplet of numbers that are always non-negative. These primaries were defined by specifying a set of curves $x(\lambda)$, $y(\lambda)$, and $z(\lambda)$, called tristimulus curves. They are shown in Figure 8(a). Using these curves, an arbitrary color C specified by its wavelenth distribution $c(\lambda)$ can be given coordinates X, Y, and Z computed as:

---

[1]

The mixing of colored lights, such as for color television, is referred to as "additive color" and its primaries are normally shades of red, green, and blue. Red and green, for example, mix to produce yellow, and all three primaries mixed equally together produce white. Mixing of paints and pigments follows similar but complementary rules and is referred to as "subtractive color". This is the basis for most color printing and photography. Its primaries are cyan (blue/green), magenta (reddish purple), and yellow. Cyan plus yellow, for example, mix to produce green, and all three mixed equally together produce black.

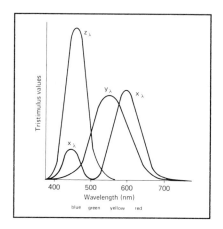 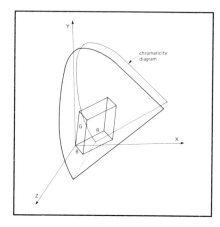

Figure 8. Tristimulus coordinates: (a) Tristimulus curves for the CIE 1931 XYZ primaries. Such curves are also called color matching curves. (b) The cone of realizable colors in XYZ space. The parallelipiped shows the range of displayable colors for a typical RGB display device.

$$X = \int c(\lambda)\, x(\lambda)\, d\lambda \qquad Y = \int c(\lambda)\, y(\lambda)\, d\lambda \qquad Z = \int c(\lambda)\, z(\lambda)\, d\lambda$$

The triplet (X, Y, Z) gives the amount of the hypothetical, non-physical primaries that would be needed to produce the color. They are called the CIE 1931 XYZ tristimulus coordinates of a color, and are among the most common means of quantitatively specifying a color. Using these values, a color is expressed as a point in the positive octant of a three dimensional space whose axes are X, Y, and Z. The $y(\lambda)$ was conveniently defined to be the Relative Luminosity Function described previously so that, in addition to being one of its tristimulus coordinates, the Y of a color gives its luminance.

If colors are considered as points in the three dimensional XYZ space, the fact that the XYZ primaries are not physically realizable means that the volume of realizable colors does not fill the space. Rather it is a type of cone, called the cone of realizable colors shown in Figure 8(b). Furthermore, any physical display device has a fixed set of primaries and can use only coefficients that are positive and have a fixed maximum, and can thus display only a subset of this cone as depicted in the figure. There is a considerable range in the phosphors used in CRTs for image and graphic displays, some al-

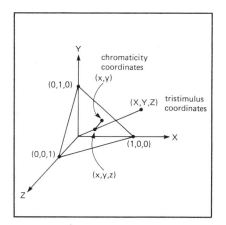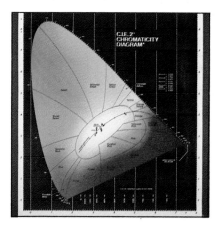

*Figure 9. Chromaticity Space: (a) The relation of chromaticity coordinates (x,y) to tristim-
ulus coordinates (X,Y,Z). (b) A chromaticity diagram. (Courtesy of Photo Research, Bur-
bank, CA. Used by permission.)*

lowing a much larger volume of this space, or range of colors, to be
displayed.

Some applications are not concerned with the luminance of a col-
or and they use chromaticity coordinates, which are defined from
tristimulus coordinates as:

$$x = \frac{X}{X + Y + Z} \quad y = \frac{Y}{X + Y + Z} \quad z = \frac{Z}{X + Y + Z}$$

Thus a given set of tristimulus coordinates has an associated set of
chromaticity coordinates, and the relation is illustrated geometrically
in Figure 9(a). Because $z = 1 - x - y$, it is redundant and is not included, and the pair (x,y) is said to specify the chromaticity of the
color. A two dimensional plot of color with chromaticity (x,y) at the
point (x,y) is known as a chromaticity diagram, as shown in
Figure 9(b), and is a standard way of representing colors. Such
plots are useful, for example, because they show the range of colors
that can be mixed by any two (those along the line joining them) or
three (those within the triangle formed by the points) given colors.

Summarizing the main points of the preceding paragraphs, we
have stated the basic experimental fact of a three color basis for col-

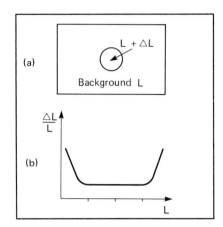

Figure 10. Brightness to luminance experiment: (a) experimental setup and (b) results.

or vision, and we have definitions for one common basis, the 1931
CIE XYZ, and for the term chromaticity.

Brightness Perception as a Function of Intensity. The derivation of the
Relative Luminosity Function did not consider how the perceived
brightness of light at a given wavelength or chromaticity changes as
the luminance or intensity is changed. Experimental results, at least
for small changes, are summarized by Weber's Law: To be just no-
ticeably different, one patch of light must exceed in luminance that
of another by a constant fraction. Thus, for an observer to just detect the pattern illustrated in Figure 10, the difference dL in luminance between the inner area and the outer area must satisfy:

$$\frac{dL}{L} = constant$$

This leads to a model for brightness of the form $B = k \log L$. As we
will see later (see Problem 3 at the end of this chapter), this model
may be used in defining transformations used for displaying images
with equally perceived brightness steps.

Chromaticity Difference Perception. Other types of experiments that
have been performed measure the sensitivity of the eye to changes in
chromaticity. Results show that, for spectral light, the eye is most
sensitive to wavelength changes in the blue/green and yellow/orange,

and least sensitive in the green and extreme red and blue. See Figure 11(a).

If the experiment is performed using colors of all chromaticities, and the results plotted on a chromaticity diagram as ellipses proportional to the variations required for a just noticeable difference (JND), the results are as in Figure 11(b). As shown in the figure, the perceptual response is variable over the range of chromaticities. This has practical implications in digital image processing. Given a color display, it shows how large a chromaticity change must be as a function of initial color to be perceived equally by an observer.

Color Perception Parameters. Although physiological evidence suggests that there are three types of cones in the eye, roughly corresponding to red, green, and blue (more correctly yellow-green, blue-green, and blue), color is not perceived as made up of these components. Rather, it is generally perceived first in terms of "color", but more precisely given the name hue (the red, green, yellow, and so on characteristic of the color), and then in other terms such as brightness, lightness, intenseness, richness, purity, and saturation. Some of these terms have been incorporated into definitions of color spaces, which are the subject of the next section.

Color Spaces

A color space is a coordinate system designed to allow colors to be measured and quantitatively specified. From tristimulus color theory, a three dimensional space is necessary, but various choices for the three coordinates are possible. Three general forms of color space coordinates are:

1. Tristimulus coordinates: A rectangular space in which the three coordinates, called the tristimulus values, give the amount of each of three fixed primaries. The recommended set of primaries are the CIE 1931 XYZ primaries, but other sets may be used. It is customary to set the scale factor so that (1,1,1) gives a reference white.

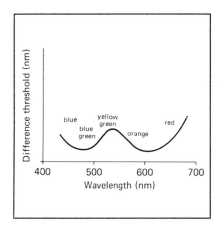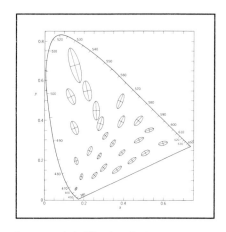

Figure 11. Sensitivity of the eye to chromaticity changes: (a) Wavelength change necessary for a JND for spectral light as a function of wavelength. (b) Ellipses proportional to the change for a JND plotted on a chromaticity diagram. (Part (b) from Wyszecki and Stiles, Color Science, Wiley and Sons, 1967, used by permission.)

2. Chromaticity coordinates: (x,y) coordinates derived from tristimulus coordinates (X,Y,Z) as described previously. To fully specify a color, its luminance Y must be specified in addition to its chromaticity.

3. Perceptual color spaces. These are color spaces based on perceptual parameters such as hue, purity, brilliance, brightness, and saturation. Many different perceptual color spaces have been defined, and a representative form is shown in Figure 12.

Some chromaticity and perceptual color spaces are defined so that the perceptual difference between two colors is given (approximately) by the Euclidean distance between the colors. In this case, the spaces are called uniform color spaces.

Within these three general types of color spaces, many specific spaces may be defined. More than 20 may be found in the literature on color and colorimetry. Some of the standard spaces are:

1. 1931 CIE XYZ and associated (x,y) chromaticities. Tristimulus coordinates X, Y, and Z, or luminance Y and chromaticity coor-

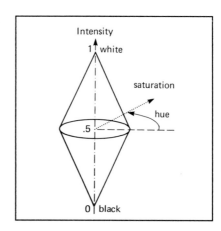

Figure 12. The form of a typical perceptual color space.

dinates (x,y) are among the most widely used references for specifying a color.

2. NTSC Receiver Primaries. NTSC refers to a set of standards for television broadcasting, and includes a set of three phosphors for color television screens. Three primaries defined by the emission characteristics of these phosphors are the axes of this tristimulus space. Notation for these primaries are R_n, G_n, B_n. Their values are assumed to range from 0 to 1, so the color space of this system is the unit cube shown in Figure 13. (Notice that all realizable colors do not fall within this cube.) A displayable color with r units of R_n, g units of G_n, and b units of B_n is represented by the point (r,g,b) in the cube. This cube is an example of the RGB color cube which we will refer to frequently in later sections. (However, we do not always require that the red, green, and blue axes be the the the NTSC red, green, and blue.)

3. $L^*u^*v^*$ (extended chromaticity). $L^*u^*v^*$ is a CIE standard space that approximates a perceptually uniform three dimensional color space. L^* is lightness, u^* is redness-greenness, and v^* is approximately blueness-yellowness. They are defined by:

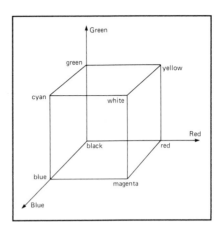

Figure 13. : R_n, G_n, B_n *color cube.*

$$L^* = 25(100\,Y/Y_0)^{1/3} - 16 \qquad Y/Y_0 \geq 0.008856$$

$$L^* = 903.3(Y/Y_0) \qquad\qquad Y/Y_0 < 0.008856$$

$$u^* = 13L^*(u' - u'_0) \qquad\qquad v^* = 13L^*(v' - v'_0)$$

where

$$u' = \frac{4X}{X + 15Y + 3Z} \qquad v' = \frac{9X}{X + 15Y + 3Z}$$

Y_0, u'_0, and v'_0 are Y, u', and v' for the reference illuminant to which the observer is adapted. This normalization for a standard illuminant is necessary because perceptually equal steps depend on the adaptation of an observer's eyes.

2.2 Monoband Image Display

We now have some properties of the human visual system, some basics of tristimulus theory, and a few color space definitions. We are ready to consider the problem of displaying an image. We assume we have an image display system, the images to display, and software facilities to read them from tape or disk and send them to the display device. The problem we consider is how to achieve a

 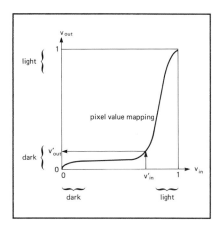

Figure 14. : Pixel value mappings. (a) Clockwise from top left: Original image, histo-gram equalization, mean and standard deviation adjustment (mean = .25, standard deviation = 0.3), and exponential adjustment based on histogram (k = 5). See explanations in text. (b) Pixel value mapping as a mapping of the interval (0,1) to (0,1). For the case shown, many of the high input values are mapped to low values, and the result will be a darker image.

pleasing display showing the interesting detail in the image; that is, how do we make the image lighter, darker, increase the contrast, and so on.

Pixel Value Mapping

We begin with the display of a single band image on a mono-chrome CRT. For the moment, let us suppose that the input pixel values are in the range (0,255). The range of values accepted by the display device may be different, say (0,63), corresponding to 6 bit data, so some form of scaling must be done. We could divide by four, which amounts to dropping off the last two bits. Value 0 will appear as black, value 63 as white, and intermediate values as shades of grey. However, even though we have scaled the data, the display may still be unsatisfactory. We describe now pixel value mapping methods, which are techniques to scale and, in general, transform the input pixel values to improve the display. The idea is illustrated by the examples of Figure 14(a).

To make the equations simpler, we will assume that both the input pixels values and the values accepted by the display device are normalized to the range (0,1). For the example above, this means we would divide the input by 255, perform the scaling, and then multiply the output by 63, performing the operations in floating point mode to keep precision. In this way, pixel value mapping can be considered as mappings of the interval (0,1) to (0,1), as shown in Figure 14(b).

The mappings are almost always implemented as table look up operations applied to the data "on the fly" as it is being displayed. That is, the pixel values of the image are not changed, but are translated as they are being sent to the display. This requires a hardware lookup table (LUT), which is now standard on almost all image processing systems. The operation is illustrated in Figure 15. Use of a lookup table is an efficient means of applying transformations because to change the display characteristics, say, the contrast or brightness, only a new table must be loaded, and not the entire image. A table only requires one entry for each possible input pixel value, say 256 for 8 bit data, whereas the image may be over one million pixels. Also, when using the table, no data is lost, as would be the case if an irreversible transformation were applied to the image. Several are mathematically irreversible, and almost all are if the clipping at the endpoints 0 and 1 is considered.

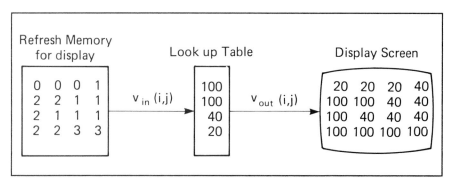

Figure 15. : Application of a pixel value transformation using a lookup table.

Examples of pixel value mappings are:

1. Linear Adjustments. These may be specified several ways.
   Gain and Bias Modification. Pixel values are transformed as:

   $$v_{out} = g\, v_{in} + b$$

   The gain g controls the contrast and the bias b controls the over-all brightness. Values of v_{out} greater than 1 are clipped to 1; values less than 0 are clipped to 0. Using this transformation, data may be scaled to the range of the display. Some examples are: (1) details in the range .5 to .6 could be spread over the entire range of the display by $g = 10$ and $b = -5.0$. Values from 0 to .50 are clipped to 0 and values greater than .60 go to 1.0; (2) $g = -1.0$ and $b = 1.0$ makes a negative of an image (black to white and white to black).

   Mean and Standard Deviation Adjustment. A mean and standard deviation may be specified for the data. The result is a linear transformation identical to the gain and bias adjustment. In this case, the gain g and bias b are computed from the specified mean and standard deviation, m_{new} and σ_{new}, and from the actual mean and standard deviation of the data, m_{data} and σ_{data}, (which must be computed) by:

   $$g = \frac{\sigma_{new}}{\sigma_{data}} \quad \text{and} \quad b = m_{new} - g\, m_{data}$$

   These results could be obtained by directly specifying the g and b, but this is often a more convenient way of specifying the parameters.

   Both of these adjustments provide the same basic capability, and the different forms are only attempts to make the adjust-ment easy for the user to specify. The best way, in fact, is to allow the user, regardless of the method, to specify the parameters in some interactive, physical way, say using a joystick, trackball or mouse. For example, for the gain/bias method, the x coordinate of a joystick may give the gain, the y the bias, and

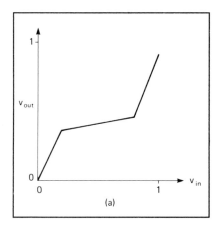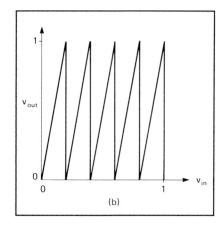

Figure 16. Piecewise linear adjustment: (a) Stretching the low and high values and compressing the middle. (b) A sawtooth adjusment.

as the joystick is moved, the stretch is computed and applied in real time.

2. Piecewise Linear Adjustments. The gain and bias modification is a linear transformation of the pixel values. This may be extended to a piecewise linear adjustment. Several sets of gs and bs are specified, each valid over a given input range. An example that stretches both the high and low pixel values while compressing the central values is shown in Figure 16(a). The adjustment can be non-continuous and/or non-monotonic, as in the sawtooth curve of Figure 16(b),

3. Thresholding or Slicing. An image may be divided into two categories by pixel value slicing, making all pixels in a range v_1 to v_2 white, and all others black. This is effective when v_1 and v_2 can be controlled interactively, say by a joystick where the x coordinate gives v_1 and the y coordinate gives v_2.

4. Logarithmic. The logarithm transformation is of the general form

$$v_{out} = \log(v_{in})$$

By including a scaling parameter k to select the portion of the logarithm curve to use, and shifting the pixels by one to avoid problems at zero, the equation becomes:

$$v_{out} = \frac{\log(1 + (e^k - 1)v_{in})}{k}$$

The effect of this transformation is to spread out the low pixel values and compress the high so that details in dark areas are made more visible at the expense of detail in the bright.

In this form, the logarithmic transformation is simply an adjustment for the visual quality of the image. However, it may have a physical meaning. In X-ray images, the value at pixel (i,j) is given by the intensity I where

$$I(i,j) = I_0 e^{-c(i,j)}$$

I_0 the intensity of the incident radiation, and $c(i,j)$ is a function of the thickness, density, and X-ray attenuation properties of the material traversed at (i,j). The logarithmic transformation is often applied to X-ray images to obtain $c(i,j)$.

5. Exponential. The inverse of the logarithmic transformation is the exponential, defined as:

$$v_{out} = e^{v_{in}}$$

It may be parameterized by allowing other bases for the exponential as:

$$v_{out} = \frac{(1 + k)^{v_{in}} - 1}{k}$$

This transformation enchances detail in the light areas, decreasing the detail in dark areas. Plots of the relation between input and output pixel values, and the effect on the image histogram for logarithmic and exponential tables are shown in Figure 17.

6. Histogram Matching. A large class of histogram modification techniques have as their objective obtaining an image histogram with a specified form. If the image originally has histogram $h_0(v_{in})$ and transformation t is applied to the pixel values giving new pixel values $v_{out} = t(v_{in})$, then a new histogram $h_1(v_{out})$ will result. Conversely, if we restrict t to be monotonic, then a given

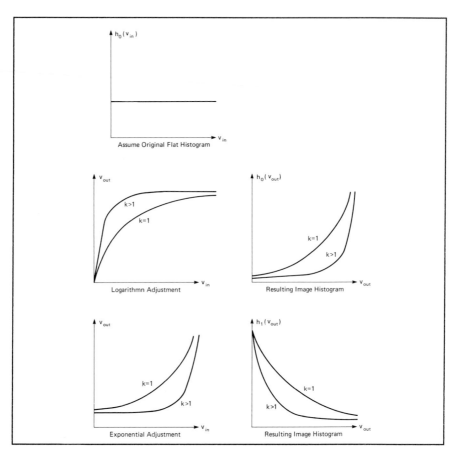

Figure 17. : Logarithmic and exponential histogram adjustments.

histogram $h_1(v_{out})$ implies a unique transformation t (ignoring truncation or clipping errors at 0 and 1) for a given original histogram $h_0(v_{in})$. If we consider the histograms as functions of a continuous variable (they are not, but are in fact defined only on integer values), then for the given image histogram $h_0(v_{in})$ and the desired histogram $h_1(v_{out})$ the transformation t must be such that:

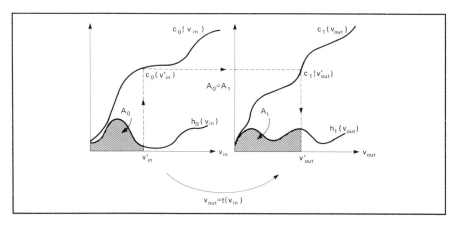

Figure 18. Pixel value mapping for histogram matching: The existing histogram on the left is to be transformed into the desired form, shown on the the right. The pixel value mapping equation is $v_{out} = c_1^{-1}(c_0(v_{in}))$.

$$\int_0^{v_{out}} h_1(u)\, du = \int_0^{v_{in}} h_0(u)\, du \qquad \text{for} \qquad v_{out} = t(v_{in})$$

This may be written as:

$$c_1(v_{out}) = c_0(v_{in})$$

where c_1 and c_0 are the cumulative histograms. For example, $c_1(v_{out})$ is the number of pixels whose value is less than or equal to v_{out}. See Figure 18. This requires that:

$$v_{out} = c_1^{-1}(c_0(v_{in})) \qquad\qquad (2.1)$$

which is the basic equation for histogram matching techniques. It is this equations that specifies how to build the tables necessary to do the matching.

7. Histogram Equalization. An important special case of histogram matching is histogram equalization, in which we want $h_1(v_{out})$ to be a constant. That is, we want an equal number of pixels in each grey level. Then

$$c_1(v_{out}) = v_{out}$$

(we have dropped a scaling constant), and by (2.1),

$$v_{out} = c_1^{-1}(c_0(v_{in}))$$
$$= c_0(v_{in})$$

This equation defines the formula for generating a table for histogram equalization, and is probably the most common pixel value mapping technique used for single band images.

An approximation that has been used above is to consider the discrete image histogram as a continuous function. Because this is not true, histogram matching cannot normally achieve an exact match. The key point is that the set of input pixel values is a discrete set, and all the pixels of a given value are mapped to the same output value. A simple example is shown in Figure 19(a). By simply using a lookup table translation of pixel values, it is impossible to achieve a histogram with 2 pixels in each of 1, 2, 3, and 4. All the pixels with value 1 will be given the same output value, and that value will never have less than 3 pixels. Mathematically, the reason is that there is no inverse for c_1 in equation 2.1, as shown in Figure 19(b) and (c). The solution for discrete data is to take as the inverse of $c_1(v_{out})$ the value of v_{out} for which $c_1(v_{out})$ is closest to $c_0(v_{in})$. Then v_{in} is mapped to v_{out} such that:

$$| c_1(v_{out}) - c_0(v_{in}) |$$

is minimum. A segment of PL/I code to do this matching in given in appendix "Software Examples" on page 197.

The histogram plots of Figure 20 illustrate this effect on an actual image. The histogram h_0 to be modified is on the left (with a single peak). Part (b) shows the histograms after the matching. Although this may look like a poor match, the jagged appearance is from the digital nature of the pixel values. If viewed as cumulative histograms, part (c), the results seem more normal.

8. Logarithmic and Exponential Adjustments based on Image Histogram. The logarithmic and exponential transformations given

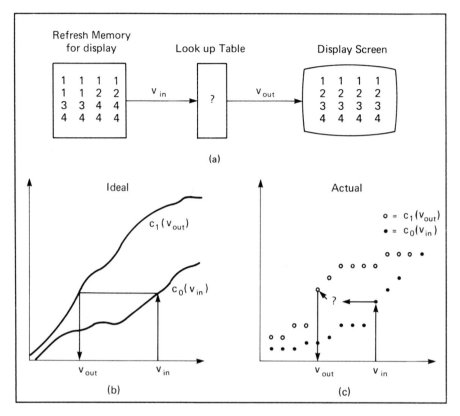

Figure 19. : *Computing the pixel value mapping for histogram matching. (a) An example showing the impossibility of exact histogram matching with table lookup. (b) The continuous histogram becomes a discrete mapping (c) with no exact inverse.*

previously do not take into account the distribution of pixels in the image. This may be included by modifying the formulas to:

$$v_{out} = \frac{\log(1 + (e^k - 1)c(v_{in}))}{k}$$

$$v_{out} = \frac{(1 + k)^{c(v_{in})} - 1}{k}$$

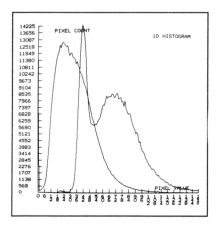

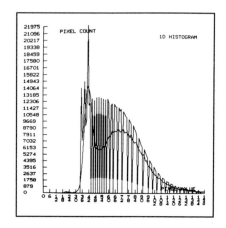

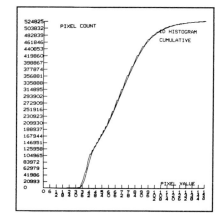

Figure 20. Before and after matched histograms: (a) The original histograms. The histogram to be modified has a single peak and is towards the left. (b) The matched histograms. (c) The matched cumulative histograms.

respectively, where $c(v_{in})$ is the normalized cumulative histogram of the image. The effect of these transformations may be considered as first performing a histogram equalization, followed by the logarithmic or exponential transformation. Except for the case of a physically based adjustment such as for X-rays, this is the normal form in which the logarithmic and exponential adjustments are applied.

The list of possible transformation can go on and on since it is clear that any function mapping (0,1) to (0,1) may be used. Often, using the different methods, surprisingly similar results are obtained, and although they are slightly different, no one is clearly better. Thus not all methods are needed in a given image processing system. What is important is to have the methods parameterized to allow user control, and the best methods of user control are those using physical variation for real time adjustments, say a joystick or mouse.

Local Pixel Value Mappings

So far, it has been assumed that a given pixel value mapping is applied to all the pixels in an image. These are called global pixel value mappings. Alternatively, the mappings may be computed locally, and varied over the image. An example of a local technique is Statistical Differencing, which tends to produce the same contrast throughout the image. Let $\overline{v(i,j)}$ and $\sigma(i,j)$ be the mean and standard deviation in some neighborhood of (i,j), say a 31 x 31 square centered on (i,j). Then

$$v_{out}(i,j) = \overline{v(i,j)} + (v_{in}(i,j) - \overline{v(i,j)})\frac{\sigma_0}{\sigma(i,j)}$$

will stretch $v_{in}(i,j)$ away from or towards the local mean to achieve a balanced local standard deviation throughout the image. σ_0 is a parameter specifying the new standard deviation, and controls the amount of stretch. In addition, the local mean can be adjusted by changing the formula to:

$$v_{out}(i,j) = \alpha m_0 + (1 - \alpha)\overline{v(i,j)} + (v_{in}(i,j) - \overline{v(i,j)})\frac{\sigma_0}{\sigma(i,j)}$$

where m_0 is the mean to force locally and α is a parameter to control the degree to which it is forced. Finally, to avoid problems when $\sigma(i,j)$ is almost 0, add the parameter β:

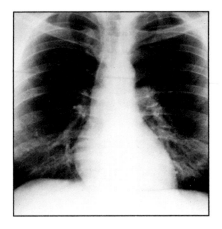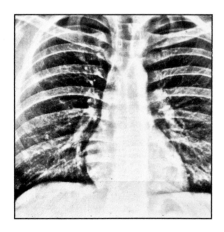

Figure 21. Statistical differencing: The input image (left) and adjusted image (right). (Data provided by Radiology Department, Brompton Hospital, London, and processed by M. Cocklin, IBM Scientific Center, UK.)

$$v_{out}(i,j) = \alpha m_0 + (1 - \alpha)\overline{v(i,j)} + (v_{in}(i,j) - \overline{v(i,j)})\frac{\beta\sigma_0}{\sigma_0 + \beta\sigma(i,j)}$$

An example of Statistical Differencing is shown in Figure 21. The input image is an X-ray, which are fairly difficult images to adjust, having a wide dynamic range and detail in both the light and dark areas.

In effect, Statistical Differencing is computing a gain and bias for each pixel in the image, and is a local form of the linear adjustment. Almost all of the other global methods may also be implemented locally. Histogram equalization, for example, when used locally, computes the new value to which $v_{in}(i,j)$ is mapped to equalize the histogram of some local neighborhood of (i,j).

The computation required for Statistical Differencing and other local methods may be significantly more than for the global methods. To help reduce this computation, a common technique is to segment the image into blocks, and exactly compute the required parameters, say the mean and standard deviation, only in each block. Linear interpolation is used between the blocks to obtain continuously varying parameters over the entire image. Alternatively, programming techniques in which the mean and standard deviations of the blocks are incrementally computed, subtracting off the old pixel values and adding on the new ones as the block is moved one column or line, allow the algorithm to be applied exactly at a reasonable cost without interpolation. The example of Figure 21 is computed exactly.

The local methods cannot be applied using the hardware lookup tables because the tables cannot be varied locally. Thus they are non-interactive, and real-time adjustment of the algorithm parameters is impossible. Nevertheless, for many images that have a large dynamic range or a strongly varying background, the local methods produce quite good results.

Pseudo Color Display Methods

The preceding section assumed one band was to be displayed as a monochromatic image on a CRT, and was concerned with techniques to redistribute the pixel values over the available levels of grey (or whatever color) to achieve enhanced displays. We now discuss ways of displaying a single band image in color. Such displays are called pseudo color displays. In this case, many more discernible levels are simultaneously available. The maximum number of discernible levels on most monochromatic displays is on the order of 50; with color, this number may easily exceed 200. Although with color there is no natural scale from low values to high, the advantage of many clearly distinguishable levels and the potential for making features stand out is important in many applications.

The slicing method described for monochrome is effective with color. In this case, a user assigns pixels in the range t_1 to t_2 to color c_1, pixels in the range t_3 to t_4 to c_2, and so on. An example is shown in Figure 22. Part (a) shows a microscope image of a virus in monochromatic grey; part (b) is the identical image with pseudocoloring. Many more details and fine structuring may be seen.

If there are many classes to be distinguished and the slices and color assignments are selected manually, the process of generating a pseudo color image becomes tedious. In general, to display a single band in color, a parametric mapping from the pixel values to coor-

Figure 22. : Monochrome and pseudocolor display of a single band image.

dinates in a color space is defined. Consider the perimeter path around the RGB cube shown in Figure 23(a). The equations for this path are:

$R(i)$	$G(i)$	$B(i)$	
1	$6i$	0	$0 \leq i < 1/6$
$1 - 6(i - 1/6)$	1	0	$1/6 \leq i < 2/6$
0	1	$6(i - 2/6)$	$2/6 \leq i < 3/6$
0	$1 - 6(i - 3/6)$	1	$3/6 \leq i < 4/6$
$6(i - 4/6)$	0	1	$4/6 \leq i < 5/6$
1	0	$1 - 6(i - 5/6)$	$5/6 \leq i \leq 6/6$

This mapping is mathematically linear (piecewise), but it is not perceptually uniform. To achieve a more perceptually uniform path, one might suppose that a mapping could be defined in one of the uniform color spaces described earlier, and this mapping transformed to the RGB color cube of the monitor. The problem is that the intersection geometry of the two spaces is often difficult to determine, and points on the path in the uniform space might fall outside the RGB cube. When truncated back into the cube, the steps will no longer be uniform. Another way to derive an approximately uniform path is to define initially a large set of equally spaced points

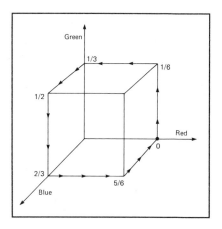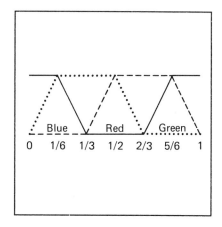

Figure 23. : Pseudo color mapping for fully saturated colors shown as the path around the RGB color cube perimeter, and as the graphs of the values of R, G, and B.

around the perimeter path in RGB, and take as the final path an equally spaced subset, as measured in a uniform space such as $L^*u^*v^*$. For example, suppose a 48 step uniform path is desired. Then define 480 equally spaced points along the perimeter in RGB. Map them to $L^*u^*v^*$, and along the path in $L^*u^*v^*$, select 48 equally spaced points. Use the corresponding 48 points in RGB as the uniform path. This method, however, has a practical problem because the chromaticities of the monitor phosphors are required, and these must be obtained from measurement. A simpler way, satisfactory for most cases, is to define the path by trial and error. Figure 24 shows a table of the RGB values derived in this way for a color wedge on a typical display. The large variation in step size for an approximately uniform path can be seen by comparing the step size in the orange and blue regions to that in the green.

2.3 Multiband Image Display

We now discuss color displays of multi-band data. We start with the most common case, displaying three bands, one each on red, green, and blue.

I	Red	Green	Blue		I	Red	Green	Blue	
01	1.000	0.000	0.000		25	0.000	0.677	1.000	
02	1.000	0.064	0.000		26	0.000	0.613	1.000	
03	1.000	0.193	0.000		27	0.000	0.548	1.000	
04	1.000	0.258	0.000		28	0.000	0.484	1.000	
05	1.000	0.323	0.000		29	0.000	0.419	1.000	
06	1.000	0.387	0.000	(o)	30	0.000	0.355	1.000	
07	1.000	0.452	0.000		31	0.000	0.290	1.000	
08	1.000	0.516	0.000		32	0.000	0.226	1.000	
09	1.000	0.548	0.000		33	0.000	0.161	1.000	
10	1.000	0.613	0.000		34	0.000	0.000	1.000	(b)
11	1.000	0.677	0.000		35	0.516	0.000	1.000	
12	1.000	0.742	0.000		36	0.581	0.000	1.000	
13	1.000	0.806	0.000		37	0.645	0.000	1.000	
14	1.000	0.871	0.000		38	0.710	0.000	1.000	
15	1.000	0.936	0.000		39	0.774	0.000	1.000	
16	1.000	1.000	0.000		40	0.839	0.000	1.000	
17	0.903	1.000	0.000		41	0.903	0.000	1.000	
18	0.806	1.000	0.000		42	0.968	0.000	1.000	
19	0.677	1.000	0.000		43	1.000	0.000	0.935	
20	0.516	1.000	0.000		44	1.000	0.000	0.839	
21	0.000	1.000	0.452	(g)	45	1.000	0.000	0.742	
22	0.000	1.000	0.710		46	1.000	0.000	0.613	
23	0.000	1.000	1.000		47	1.000	0.000	0.484	
24	0.000	0.871	1.000		48	1.000	0.000	0.097	

Figure 24. : RGB values for an approximately uniform 48 step path aroung the perimeter of the color cube derived by trial-and-error. Notice the variation in the step size along the path. Large steps are found in green, around the (g), small steps in orange (o) and blue (b).

RGB Image Display

A display of a three band image in which one band is applied to the red gun, one to the green, and one to the blue is called an RGB display. An example is shown in Figure 25.

In some cases, three bands of an image are available corresponding to the red, green, and blue hues. If so, these can be displayed on the corresponding guns of a color CRT to give a natural color image. To reproduce true colors, the XYZ coordinates (or equivalent) of the bands, the XYZ components of the CRT phosphors, and the response curves of the generating process and display device must be known. True color reproduction may not be possible depending on these parameters. Fortunately, in most cases, true color reproduction is not critical and the red, green, and blue components are displayed without regard to exact color reproduction.

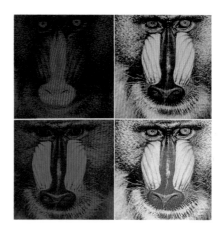

Figure 25. : Red, green, and blue components and a full color RGB image.

Another case occurs when bands are available that do not correspond to red, green, and blue. Images from infrared and multispectral photography and multispectral satellite scanners are examples. Since the data may represent radiation in infrared or microwave wavelengths, true color is meaningless. In this case, the displays of the bands in red, green, and blue are called false color displays. The choice of which band to display on which color gun is somewhat arbitrary. In cases for which the bands correspond to spectral bands, they are often assigned to the red, green, and blue guns from the longest wavelength to the shortest. In cases where the bands represent derived components such as ratios of bands or principal components, (appendix "Principal Components" on page 192), no widely adopted conventions exist. The objective is to present the maximum information to an observer.

Each band of a false color display may be adjusted independently using any of the pixel value mapping methods described for monoband displays. For example, histogram equalization or logarithmic transformations may be applied. This is the most common approach to adjusting displayed colors. Often satisfactory results can be obtained in this way. However, sooner or later, a difficult scene seems to arrive for which it is hard to get a good display, and in the process of trying, several characteristics of the RGB display method are noticed:

1. Adjustments to one band affect many colors and perceived characteristics of the display. An increase in the gain applied to the red band increases the brightness for all pixels with a red component (purple, magenta, and so on) and not just the pure red. Also, it decreases the saturation of cyan (green plus blue) by shifting it to white, and decreases the amount of green by converting it to yellow (red plus green).
2. It is difficult to control perceptual properties of the image. For example, in an RGB display, it is difficult to increase the overall saturation to get brigher colors. Increasing all three tends to give more white.
3. In the case that the three bands to be displayed are highly correlated with each other, RGB displays are typically flat and have a large grey component. This is because the correlated pixels lie in an area, very roughly ellipsoidal, near the $R = G = B$ diagonal as shown in Figure 26(a). Techniques such as histogram equalization or linear transformations of the individual bands elongate or tilt the ellipsoid, part (b), but do not cause it to expand to fill the available color space.

There are several methods that may be tried to overcome these problems. The next section describes techniques of color decorrelation which are often an effective way of solving the third problem above. Following that is a description of some non-RGB color spaces which may be used to avoid some of the perceptual problems.

Color Decorrelation for RGB Displays

Much of the flatness and greyness of some RGB displays is due to the correlation between the bands. Different spectral bands gathered by earth sensing satellites and images from astronomy studies of similar wavelengths are typical of highly correlated data, and what is needed is a way to remove this correlation; that is, a way to ex-

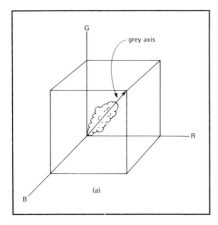 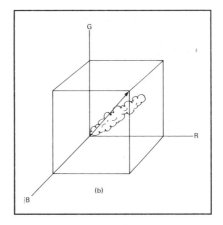

Figure 26. : (a) Spread of pixel values in RGB for typical correlated bands. (b) Effect of independently stretching one band. The data is not stretched to fill the color cube by this operation.

pand the distribution away from the grey axis out into the "corners" of the RGB color cube.

One method is a direct three dimensional histogram equalization. This is not an easy problem, in some respects similar to the *n*-body problem of classical mechanics. An approximate method may be used that repeatedly stretches the three two dimensional histograms. Let the three bands to be displayed be denoted as R, G, and B, and let RG, GB, and BR be the two dimensional histograms. Then by iteratively applying the steps:

    1.   For each value of *r* in RG, spread the *g* values.
    2.   For each value of *g* in GB, spread the *b* values.
    3.   For each value of *b* in BR, spread the *r* values.

the data is spread out to fill the color cube. The iteration is necessary because only a partial stretch is applied at any one time to avoid discontinuities in the color assignments that would result if pixels originally close to each other were mapped to colors far apart. A result of the method is shown in Figure 27.

Another approach [8] is to compute the principal component axes of the original three dimensional pixel value distribution, shown

Figure 27. : Before and after color decorrelation by 3d histogram equalization.

in Figure 28, and stretch in the direction of these axes, but keep the data in RGB space for the display. In this way, the distribution may be changed from a narrow, approximately ellipsoidal shape into a more-or-less uncorrelated spherical shape, providing a more uniform distribution of points throughout RGB space. Conceptually, the data transformation which must be applied is:

1. Transform the data in its principal components.
2. Stretch (equalize) each principal component; that is, stretch along the axes of the ellipsoid in principal component space.
3. Transform the data back to the original space.

These operations may be combined into a single linear transformation for each band. In matrix form, the equation is:

$$D' = D E S E^{-1}$$

D is the $n \times 3$ matrix of pixel values to be displayed (three components, r, g, and b, for each of n pixels, where n is the total number of pixels in the image), E is the matrix whose columns are the eigenvectors of $D^T D$, S is a diagonal scaling matrix, and D' is the computed result, an $n \times 3$ matrix of the new r, g, b values for each of the n pixels. Thus each column of D and D' is a complete band of an

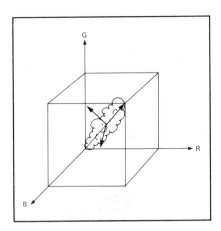

Figure 28. : Axes computed by the method of principal components are shown. By stretching along these axes, the data is moved towards the corners of the color cube.

image, strung out into a one dimensional array. The matrix S scales the values in the space of principal components. Considering the operations as proceeding from the left, the pixel values in D are transformed to principal components by E, scaled by S, then transformed back to the original space by E^{-1}.

Figure 29 shows a satellite image in standard RGB color before and after this type of color decorrelation, and two dimensional histogram of two of the bands used in the display. In this case, the scaling matrix S was:

$$S = \begin{pmatrix} s_1\dfrac{\sigma_1}{\sigma_1} & 0 & 0 \\ 0 & s_2\dfrac{\sigma_1}{\sigma_2} & 0 \\ 0 & 0 & s_3\dfrac{\sigma_1}{\sigma_3} \end{pmatrix}$$

where the s_i are user entered parameters to control the scaling and σ_i is the standard deviation in the i-th principal component. Simply equalizing the standard deviations ($s_i = 1$) tends to be too severe and enhances the noise in the second and third components. For the results shown, $s_1 = 1$, $s_2 = 0.5$, and $s_3 = 0.2$.

An advantage of these decorrelation methods which is perhaps not so obvious is that the resulting displays are in the same general color representation as the original data. The other color spaces and

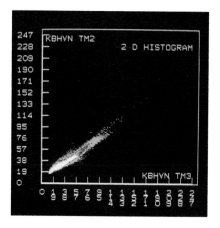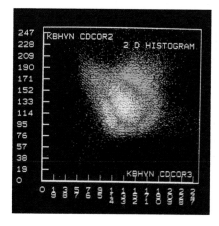

*Figure 29. Principal component color decorrelation: Top: Before and after RGB displays.
Bottom: Before and after two dimensional histograms for two of the three bands used in the
displays.*

display modes we will discuss next present the data in a significantly
different way that can be hard to interpret. For example, crops that
appear red (not green!) in the standard RGB false color displays of
satellite multispectral data may appear as another color. In color
decorrelation, the basic color scheme does not change, and the user's
experience in interpreting the image still applies.

Display methods other than RGB are based on adopting another color space and assigning the bands to be displayed to the coordinates in this space. The physical display device must still be driven by signals for RGB, so the transformation from the new color space to RGB must be done as shown in Figure 30.

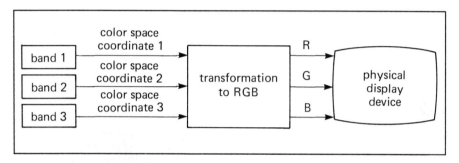

Figure 30.   Using an alternate color space on an RGB device.

If a perceptually uniform space is needed, one possibility is to use the *L*u*v** space. Section "Color Spaces" on page 31 listed the defining equations. The inverse equations mapping to RGB are in two steps, *L*u*v** to XYZ, and XYZ to RGB:

$$Y = 0.01\left(\frac{L^* + 16}{25}\right)^3$$

$$X = \frac{9(u^* + 13v'_0 L^*)}{4(v^* + 13v'_0 L^*)}Y$$

$$Z = \left(\frac{39L^*}{(v^* + 13v'_0 L^*)} - 5\right)Y - \frac{X}{3}$$

$$R = 1.86X - 0.52Y - 0.28Z$$

$$G = 0.98X + 2.0\ Y - 0.028Z$$

$$B = 0.064X - 0.129Y + 0.98Z$$

The last three equations assume an NTSC standard monitor. To be accurately used on a given monitor, the XYZ coordinates of the phosphors of the monitor must be obtained by measurement. To result in displayable colors using these equations, (RGB in the range (0,1)), the data assigned to $L^*u^*v^*$ must have approximate means and standard deviations [9]:

$$\overline{L^*} = 61 \qquad \overline{u^*} = 15 \qquad \overline{v^*} = 6$$
$$\sigma_{L^*} = 61 \qquad \sigma_{u^*} = 49 \qquad \sigma_{v^*} = 16$$

The above transformation equations are not so simple, and in many cases the precise properties of the space are not needed. Other color spaces have been defined that are similar to perceptual color spaces or that have simple computational transformations. Two of these are:

1. Intensity, Hue, and Saturation (IHS) spaces. IHS spaces match a common form of perceptual space, the one that was shown in Figure 12 on page 33. When defined for an RGB display system, intensity I is measured along the central $R = G = B$ diagonal of the color cube. Hue H and saturation S are polar coordinates in the plane perpendicular to the I diagonal. The hue angle is measured from some arbitrarily selected direction such as blue or red, and S is the radial distance out to the color.
    Figure 31 illustrates the geometry. If we set $H = 0$ in the direction of blue, the transformation equations from IHS to RGB may be derived from the figure. The intensity axis I is $R = G = B$, the vector v_1 is orthogonal to I in the plane of I and B, and v_2 is the vector $I \times v_1$ to complete the orthogonal system. The transformation is:

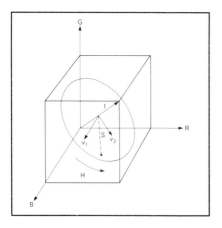 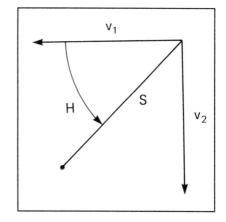

Figure 31. IHS coordinates within the RGB cube: (a) The I, v_1, and v_2 axes in the RGB cube, and (b) converting from v_1, and v_2 to H and S.

$$\begin{pmatrix} I \\ v_1 \\ v_2 \end{pmatrix} = \begin{pmatrix} 1/3 & 1/3 & 1/3 \\ -1/\sqrt{6} & -1/\sqrt{6} & 2/\sqrt{6} \\ 1/\sqrt{6} & -2/\sqrt{6} & 0 \end{pmatrix} \begin{pmatrix} R \\ G \\ B \end{pmatrix} \qquad [2.2]$$

v_1 and v_2 are converted to a polar coordinate system giving H and S to complete the transformation:

$$H = \tan^{-1}\left(\frac{v_2}{v_1}\right) \text{ in the range 0 to 360} \qquad \text{and} \qquad S = \sqrt{v_1^2 + v_2^2}$$

To use the IHS coordinates for display, it is the inverse transform that is required. In matrix form, this is given by:

$$\begin{pmatrix} R \\ G \\ B \end{pmatrix} = \begin{pmatrix} 1 & -0.204124 & 0.612372 \\ 1 & -0.204124 & -0.612372 \\ 1 & 0.408248 & 0 \end{pmatrix} \begin{pmatrix} I \\ v_1 \\ v_2 \end{pmatrix}$$

where

$$v_1 = S \cos 2\pi H \qquad \text{and} \qquad v_2 = S \sin 2\pi H$$

59

Several variations on this system are common. One is to define the vector dot product between two colors R_1, G_1, B_1 and R_2, G_2, B_2 as the weighted product:

$$.30\ R_1\ R_2 + .59\ G_1\ G_2 + .11\ B_1\ B_2$$

The coefficients are taken from the luminosities of the phosphors of an NTSC standard monitor, and weight the hues by their perceived brightness. For these coefficients, $(1,1,1)$ is a unit vector. Defining the I orthogonal plane as orthogonal under this dot product, the planes of constant I approximate planes of constant brightness. Geometrically, the effect is that the planes of constant I are tilted with respect to the I axis. The transformation from RGB to IHS becomes:

$$\begin{pmatrix} I \\ v_1 \\ v_2 \end{pmatrix} = \begin{pmatrix} .3 & .59 & .11 \\ -.105465 & -.207424 & .312889 \\ 0.445942 & -.445942 & 0 \end{pmatrix} \begin{pmatrix} R \\ G \\ B \end{pmatrix}$$

where the transformation to polar coordinates is the same. The inverse transform necessary for display is:

$$\begin{pmatrix} R \\ G \\ B \end{pmatrix} = \begin{pmatrix} 1 & -.351561 & 1.486587 \\ 1 & -.351561 & -.755857 \\ 1 & 2.484450 & 0 \end{pmatrix} \begin{pmatrix} I \\ v_1 \\ v_2 \end{pmatrix} \qquad [2.3]$$

A color wheel in IHS, with constant $I = 0.5$, hue in angle, and S radially, is shown in Figure 32. In part (a), the plane of constant I is orthogonal to the I axis, and in (b), the tilted plane is used. The figure shows that the tilted plane version more nearly corresponds to the natural idea of constant intensity.

An additional variation computes S in the interval $(0,1)$ and, because the possible values S that stay inside the color cube depend on I and H, S is specified as a percentage of its maximum possible value for a given I and H. In this case, the transformations become:

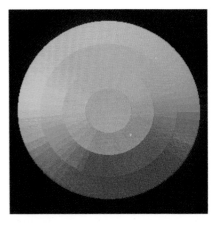 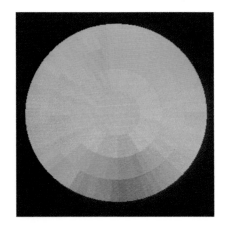

Figure 32. A plane of constand I in (a) a non-tilted and (b) a tilted IHS space.

$$\begin{pmatrix} \sigma_1 \\ \sigma_2 \\ \sigma_3 \end{pmatrix} = M^{-1} \begin{pmatrix} 0 \\ \cos\ 2\pi H \\ \sin\ 2\pi H \end{pmatrix}$$

$$S_{top} = -\min_i(0, \sigma_i) \qquad S_{bot} = \max_i(0, \sigma_i) \qquad S_{globalmax} = \frac{1}{S_{top} + S_{bot}}$$

$$I_{maxsat} = S_{top} \times S_{globalmax}$$

$$S_{localmax} = \begin{cases} S_{globalmax} \times \dfrac{I}{I_{maxsat}} & \text{if } I < I_{maxsat} \\[2ex] S_{globalmax} \times \dfrac{1-I}{1-I_{maxsat}} & \text{if } I \geq I_{maxsat} \end{cases}$$

$$\begin{pmatrix} R \\ G \\ B \end{pmatrix} = \begin{pmatrix} I \\ I \\ I \end{pmatrix} + S \times S_{localmax} \times \begin{pmatrix} \sigma_1 \\ \sigma_2 \\ \sigma_3 \end{pmatrix}$$

I_{maxsat} is the value of I for which the given H can have its maximum saturation, and $S_{globalmax}$ is this maximum saturation. $S_{localmax}$ is the maximum possible saturation of H at the intensity I. The matrix M^{-1} is the matrix given above in equation 2.3. PL/I code for this tranformation, and for the inverse transformation

61

from RGB to IHS is given in "RGB to IHS Transformation in PL/I" on page 206.

It turns out that displays with high values of S are generally more pleasing than those with low values. In fact, setting S to 1, its maximum value, and using only I and H provides an effective display method when only two bands are available.

2. Hue, Lightness, and Saturation (HLS). The HLS space [11] is a system recommended for computer graphics by the Graphics Standards Committee, Siggraph, ACM. H is in the range (0,360) with $H = 0$ blue, and $L, S, R, G,$ and B are in the range (0,1). The transformations are:

HLS to RGB

If $L \leq 0.5$ *then*
   $M = L(1+S)$
Else
   $M = L+S-L*S$
Endif
$m = 2 \times L - M$
$R = Value(m,M,H)$
$G = Value(m,M,H-120)$
$B = Value(m,M,H-240)$
Endif

where $Value(m,M,h)$ *is defined as:*

If $h < 0$ *then*
   $h = h + 360$
Endif
If $h < 60$ *then*
   $Value = m + (M-m)*h/60$
Elseif $h < 180$ *then*
   $Value = M$
Elseif $h < 240$ *then*

RGB to HLS

$M = max(R,G,B)$
$m = min(R,G,B)$
If $M / = m$ *then*
   $r = (M\text{-}R)/(M\text{-}m)$
$g = (M\text{-}G)/(M\text{-}m)$
$b = (M\text{-}B)/(M\text{-}m)$
(Else
   $R=G=B$ *and* $r,g,$ *and* b
   are not needed.)

(Note that at least one of r,b,g is 0 and at least one is 1.)
$L = (M+m)/2$
If $M = m$ *then*
   $S = 0$
Else
   If $L <= 0.5$ *then*
     $S = (M\text{-}m)/(M+m)$
   Else
     $S = (M\text{-}m)/(2\text{-}M\text{-}m)$
   Endif

$Value = m + (M\text{-}m)*(240\text{-}h)/60$

Else

   $Value = m$

Endif

$Endif$

$If\ S=0\ then$

   $h=0$

$Elseif\ R=M\ then$

   $h=2+b\text{-}g$

$Elseif\ G=M\ then$

   $h=4+r\text{-}b$

$Else$

   $h=6+g\text{-}r$

$Endif$

Figure 33 shows examples of an IHS, an IH, and an HLS display.

Problems in Using non-RGB Color Spaces. Several problems are encountered when using the non-RGB color spaces.

1. The pixel value mapping method used for a component of a color space depends on how the color space maps onto the RGB cube. In IHS, some values of I allow many values of H and S, while others allow only few. See Figure 34(c). Histogram equalization may be suitable for single band monochrome displays and for RGB displays of uncorrelated data, but it groups the same number of levels in the black and white regions, where there are few values of hue and saturation, as in the middle portion where there are many more. IHS displays using histogram equalization typically look stark and overly contrasted. A better distribution for I is one in which the number of points at intensity I is proportional to the area of the polygon of intersection of the I orthogonal plane and the RGB cube. This is given by:

$$h(I) \sim \begin{cases} I^{\frac{3}{2}} & 0 \leq I \leq 1/3 \text{ and } 2/3 \leq I \leq 1 \\ -(I-1/2)^2 & 1/3 \leq I \leq 2/3 \end{cases}$$

For S, a standard histogram equalization produces too many values close to the I axis where all hues have a similar grey. A better distribution is one that increases with increasing S, proportional to the perimeter of the polygon. The shapes for these

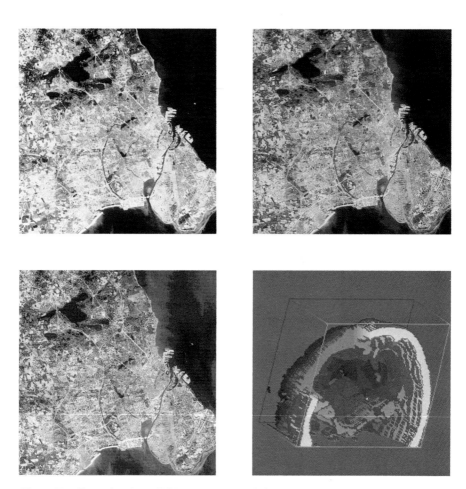

Figure 33. Examples of non-RGB color spaces: (a) An RGB display of a three band satellite image. (b) An IHS display of the first three principal components of the data displayed in (a). (c) An IH display of only the first two components, with the saturation set to the maximum. For completeness, we could have shown displays of the original bands in IHS, and of principal components in RGB, but these do not produce pleasing displays and are not often used. (d) An HLS display in which L is varied to give the impression of depth in a medical tomography image. (Data part for (d) provided by Drs. R. A. Zappula and W. C. Yang of Mt. Sinai School of Medicine, processed by Ed Farrell, IBM T. J. Watson Research Center, New York.)

histograms are shown in Figure 34(d), and a comparison of images displayed in IHS with histogram equalization and with these distributions is shown in (a) and (b).

2. The number of levels of each of R, G, and B is fixed by the hardware of a given display device, but the number of levels for each coordinate of a non-RGB space is set in the software. These can be chosen arbitrarily so long as the total number of displayable colors remains less than or equal to the total number possible on the device. Changing the number of levels may produce a significant effect on resulting displays. If $n_r = n_g = n_b = 16$, (n_r is the number of levels of red, etc.) a total of $16^3 = 4096$ colors are displayable. If an IHS color space is to be used, two examples of ways of assigning the levels are:

	I	H	S	Total
1.	16	16	16	4096
2.	16	64	4	4096

Color wheels using these two ways are shown in Figure 35. Using 16-64-4, more hues are available, and less levels of saturation. In general, this is more satisfying because the eye prefers a broad range of hues to a broad range of saturations.

2.4   Discussion

Although it is not always easy, and may require some trial-and-error, good displays can be obtained for most images if a choice of display methods is available. For monochrome displays, the main factor is the choice of the pixel value mapping, and several methods should be available. These are best if controlled interactively by a joystick. For color displays, an additional factor is the choice of color space, and both an RGB and a perceptual-type such as IHS are useful. For the non-RGB color spaces, the pixel value mapping method applied to the components should match the geometry of the components' intersection with the RGB cube. For multiband color displays, uncorrelated data generally produces more pleasing results,

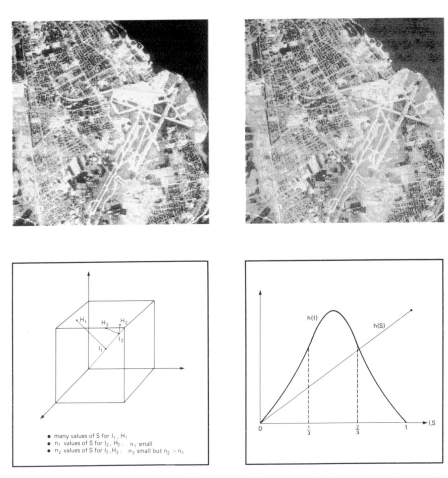

Figure 34. Pixel value mapping for IHS.: (a) IHS display with histogram equalization for each of I, H, and S. (b) IHS display using the I and S histograms of part (d). (c) Examples showing how the number of S values depend on the values of I and H. (d) Histograms for I and S to partially overcome the problem shown in (c). They were derived to better match the geometry of the IHS mapping onto the RGB cube.

and correlated data may need special processing such as color decorrelation to avoid flat, greyish displays.

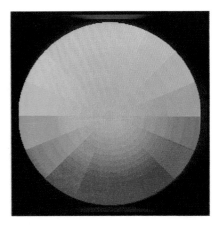 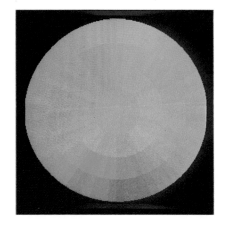

Figure 35. : *Effect of the number of levels assigned to each of I, H, and S. (a) 16-16-16. (b) 16-64-4.*

2.5 Questions and Problems

1. Given three bands with the histograms shown below, what will the resulting display look like if they are displayed in RGB?

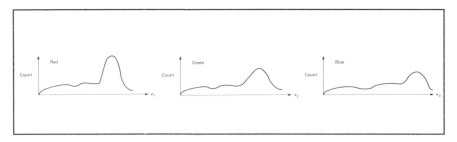

Figure 36. : *Histograms for three bands for an RGB display.*

2. Assume that an HLS coordinate system will be used to display images on an RGB device. What form should the histogram have for the L component in the HLS model so that the number of points in each level of L is proportional to the number of different displayable colors at that level?

3. (Histogram hyperbolization [5]). Derive the equation for a pixel value mapping that will produce an equalized brightness im-

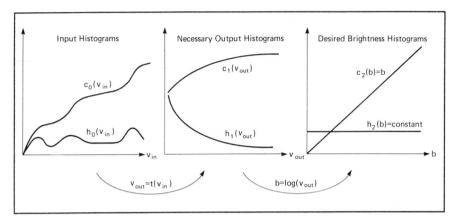

Figure 37. : *Histograms and cumulative distributions for histogram hyperbolization.*

age; that is, one with an equal number of pixels displayed in each perceived brightness level. Assume brightness and pixel value are related by Weber's Law. What is the form of the pixel value histogram? Which pixel value mapping described in Section "Pixel Value Mapping" on page 35 does it most closely resemble?

To get you started, see Figure 37. You want $h_2(b) = k$, where $h_2(b)$ the histogram computed over brightness levels, and k is a constant. This means $c_2(b) = b$ where we are ignoring a scaling constant. Find the histogram computed over pixel values that will give this distribution for brightness.

4. We listed two ways of specifying a linear pixel value mapping, one specifying directly the gain and bias, the other a mean and standard deviation. Give the equations for a linear pixel value mapping in which a user specifies the two values v_{min} and v_{max} $(v_{min} < v_{max})$ which are mapped to 0 and 1 respectively.

5. Using Figure 31, derive equation 2.5, converting from RGB to IHS coordinates.

3.0 Filtering

In this chapter we consider techniques for filtering digital images. This includes both low pass (smoothing) and high pass (edge enhancement) filters. The type of filters we discuss are called "enhancement filters" as opposed to "reconstruction filters". A reconstruction filter attempts to restore an image based on some knowledge of the degradation it has undergone, whereas an enhancement filter attempts to improve the quality of an image for human or machine interpretability, where quality is measured subjectively. Most enhancement filters are heuristic and problem oriented, and models of the degradation are generally not used in deriving them.

We begin with an outline of one result from linear systems theory describing linear filters, and this will lead to digital convolution and the moving window operation common in digital image filtering.

3.1 Digital Convolution and Moving Window Operations

Linear systems theory is a branch of mathematics used to describe optical systems and electrical circuits and it provides the mathematical basis for certain filters used in digital image processing. A system S is considered a black box with an input $f(x)$ and output $g(x) = S(f(x))$:

$$f(x) \longrightarrow S \longrightarrow g(x)$$

In our case, $f(x)$ is the original image, represented in one dimension for simplicity, $g(x)$ the filtered output image, and S the filtering operation. The result we want from linear systems theory is that if a filter satisfies certain conditions (if it is linear and shift invariant), then output of the filter can be expressed mathematically in the simple form:

$$g(x) = \int f(t) \, h(x - t) \, dt \qquad (3.1)$$

where $h(t)$, called the point spread function or impulse response, is a function that completely characterizes the filter. The integral expression is a common form called a convolution integral and is written in short as $g = f*h$.

In the digital case, the integral becomes a summation:

$$g(i) = \sum_{k=-\infty}^{+\infty} f(k) \, h(i - k) \qquad (3.2)$$

and, although the limits on the summation are infinite, the function h is usually zero outside some range, such as the examples of Figure 38.

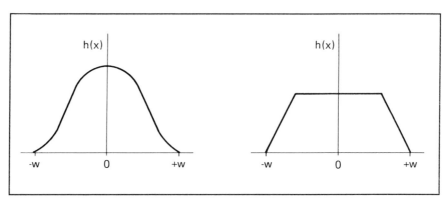

Figure 38. Form of a typical point spread function $h(t)$.

If the range over which h is non zero is $(-w, +w)$, then equation (3.2) may be written as:

$$g(i) = \sum_{k=i-w}^{i+w} f(k)\, h(i-k) \tag{3.3}$$

This says that the output $g(i)$ at point i is given by a weighted sum of input pixels surrounding i where the weights are given by the $h(k)$. To create the output at the next pixel $i+1$ the function $h(k)$ is shifted by one, and the weighted sum is recomputed. The full output is created by a series of shift-multiply-sum operations, and this is called a digital convolution. In two dimensions, $h(k)$ becomes $h(k,l)$ and equation (3.3) becomes a double summation:

$$g(i,\ j) = \sum_{k=i-w}^{i+w} \sum_{l=j-v}^{j+v} f(k,l) h(i-k,\ j-l)$$

Here again, $g(i,\ j)$ is created by a series of shift-multiply-sum operations as illustrated in Figure 39. The values of h are also referred to as the filter weights, the filter kernel, or the filter mask[2]. For reasons of symmetry, $h(i,\ j)$ is almost always chosen to be of size $m \times n$ where both m and n are odd. Often $m = n$.

In some cases, h may be represented as the vector outer product of a vertical component vector $h_v(l)$ and a horizontal component vector $h_h(m)$:

$$h(l,m) = h_v(l)\, h_h(m)^T$$

If so, then h is called separable. This will become clear in some examples below. Separability is an important property computationally because it means that the filter may be applied by first convolving the image with the horizontal component h_h and then convolving the result with the vertical component h_v (or vice versa). This replaces a two dimensional convolution with two one dimen-

---

2

  There is a reflection between the filter weights and the point spread function of a filter. If $h(k,l)$ is the point spread function, then the weights or filter mask is usually given as $h(-k, -l)$.

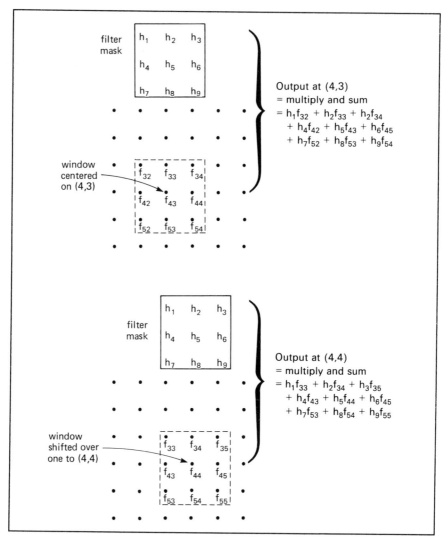

Figure 39. Digital Convolution: The output at a point is given by the sum of the input values around the point, each multiplied by the corresponding term of the h array. To compute the next output value, the h array is shifted, and the multiply and sum operation repeated.

sional convolutions, reducing the computation from the order of n^2 to the order of $2n$.

In physical systems, the kernel h must be always non-negative, which results in some blurring or averaging of the image. The narrower h, the better the system, in the sense of less blurring. In digital image processing, h may be defined arbitrarily (remember the flexibility we spoke of in the introduction) and this gives rise to many types of filters. In fact, by extending the basic idea of convolution, the weights of h may be varied over the image, and the size and shape of the window varied. These operations are no longer linear, and are no longer convolutions, but become general "moving window operations" which are very common in digital image processing. With this flexibility, a wide range of linear, non-linear, and adaptive filters may be implemented such as for edge enhancement or selective smoothing.

3.2 Digital Approximations to the Gradient and Laplacian

Before proceding to smoothing filters, we describe the gradient and Laplacian operators. These are two filters, in fact, two classes of filters, that are often applied to digital images as convolutions. They are related to the vector gradient and scalar Laplacian of calculus. These are defined for a continuous function $f(x,y)$ of two variables as:

$$\text{Gradient:} \quad \nabla f = \frac{\partial f}{\partial x}\bar{i} + \frac{\partial f}{\partial y}\bar{j} \qquad \text{Laplacian:} \quad \nabla^2 f = \frac{\partial^2 f}{\partial x^2} + \frac{\partial^2 f}{\partial y^2}$$

where $\bar{i}$ and $\bar{j}$ are unit vectors in the x and y directions.

Gradient. The gradient operator applied to a continuous function produces a vector at each point whose direction gives the direction of maximum change of the function at that point, and whose magnitude gives the magnitude of this maximum change. A digital gradient may be computed by convolving two windows with an image, one window giving the x component g_x of the gradient, and the other giving the y component g_y:

$$g_x(i, j) = mask_x * n(i, j) \qquad g_y(i, j) = mask_y * n(i, j)$$

where $n(i, j)$ is some neighborhood of (i, j) and * represents the sum of products of the corresponding terms. The simplest set of masks is:

$$mask_x = -1 \quad 1 \qquad mask_y = \begin{matrix} -1 \\ 1 \end{matrix}$$

giving

$$g_x(i, j) = v(i, j+1) - v(i, j)$$

$$g_y(i, j) = v(i+1, j) - v(i, j)$$

This $mask_x$ generates output values centered on the point $(i, j+1/2)$ and the $mask_y$ generates output values centered on $(i+1/2, j)$. To obtain values centered on (i, j), masks symmetric about (i, j) are most often used. To get

$$g_x(i, j) = v(i, j+1) - v(i, j-1)$$

$$g_y(i, j) = v(i+1, j) - v(i-1, j)$$

the masks

$$mask_x = -1 \quad 0 \quad 1 \qquad \text{and} \qquad mask_y = \begin{matrix} -1 \\ 0 \\ 1 \end{matrix}$$

are used. Other common masks are:

$$mask_x = \begin{pmatrix} -1 & 0 & 1 \\ -2 & 0 & 2 \\ -1 & 0 & 1 \end{pmatrix} \quad mask_y = \begin{pmatrix} -1 & -2 & -1 \\ 0 & 0 & 0 \\ 1 & 2 & 1 \end{pmatrix} \quad \text{(Sobel operators)}$$

$$mask_x = \begin{pmatrix} -1 & 0 & 1 \\ -1 & 0 & 1 \\ -1 & 0 & 1 \end{pmatrix} \quad mask_y = \begin{pmatrix} -1 & -1 & -1 \\ 0 & 0 & 0 \\ 1 & 1 & 1 \end{pmatrix} \quad \text{(Prewitt operators)}$$

Typical gradient masks for a larger window are:

$$mask_x = \begin{pmatrix} -1/4 & -1/3 & 0 & 1/3 & 1/4 \\ -1/3 & -1/2 & 0 & 1/2 & 1/3 \\ -1/2 & -1 & 0 & 1 & 1/2 \\ -1/3 & -1/2 & 0 & 1/2 & 1/3 \\ -1/4 & -1/3 & 0 & 1/3 & 1/4 \end{pmatrix} \qquad mask_y = \begin{pmatrix} -1/4 & -1/3 & -1/2 & -1/3 & -1/4 \\ -1/3 & -1/2 & -1 & -1/2 & -1/3 \\ 0 & 0 & 0 & 0 & 0 \\ 1/3 & 1/2 & 1 & 1/2 & 1/3 \\ 1/4 & 1/3 & 1/2 & 1/3 & 1/4 \end{pmatrix}$$

Sometimes the gradient is wanted as a magnitude g_m and an angle g_a. These can be computed from g_x and g_y as:

$$g_m(i,\ j) = \sqrt{g_x^2 + g_y^2} \qquad or \qquad g_m(i,\ j) = |g_x| + |g_y|$$

$$g_a(i,\ j) = \tan^{-1}\left(\frac{g_y}{g_x}\right)$$

Another set of masks, called the Robert's operators, are not oriented along the x- and y- direction, but are nevertheless similar. They are defined on a 2 x 2 window as:

$$mask_1 = \begin{pmatrix} 1 & 0 \\ 0 & -1 \end{pmatrix} \qquad\qquad mask_2 = \begin{pmatrix} 0 & 1 \\ -1 & 0 \end{pmatrix}$$

Whatever masks are used, the gradient operator produces a two element vector at each pixel, and this is usually stored as two new images, one for each component.

Laplacian. The Laplacian operator, which in one dimension reduces to the second derivative, is also computed by convolving a mask with the image. One of the masks that is used may be derived by comparing the continuous and digital cases as follows:

Continuous	*Digital*
$f(x)$	$v(i)$
$f'(x)$	$v'(i) = v(i) - v(i-1)$
$f''(x) = \nabla^2 f(x)$	$v''(i) = v'(i) - v'(i-1)$

$$= [v(i) - v(i-1)] - [v(i-1) - v(i-2)]$$
$$= v(i-2) - 2v(i-1) - v(i)$$
$$= (1 \quad -2 \quad 1)(v(i-2)\ \ v(i-1)\ \ v(i)) \qquad (3.4)$$

giving the convolution mask $(1 \quad -2 \quad 1)$. In this form, the Laplacian at i is computed from values centered about $i-1$. To keep the Laplacian symmetric, it is normally shifted and given at i as:

$$(1 \quad -2 \quad 1) \quad (v(i-1) \quad v(i) \quad v(i+1))$$

Also, the sign is typically changed to give:

$$(-1 \quad 2 \quad -1) \quad (v(i-1) \quad v(i) \quad v(i+1))$$

and this is a common form of the one dimensional digital Laplacian although mathematically it is the negative of the Laplacian. Different choices are available when extending this mask to two dimensions. Two standard masks are:

$$\begin{matrix} & -1 & \\ -1 & 4 & -1 \\ & -1 & \end{matrix} \qquad \begin{matrix} -1 & -1 & -1 \\ -1 & 8 & -1 \\ -1 & -1 & -1 \end{matrix}$$

Again, this is the negative of the mathematical Laplacian.

A further result may be seen by rewriting the terms in equation (3.4) to give:

$$\begin{aligned} \nabla^2 v(i) &= 3v(i) - (v(i-1) + v(i) + v(i+1)) \\ &= 3v(i) - 3(local\ mean\ at\ i) \end{aligned} \tag{3.5}$$

showing that the Laplacian at i is proportional to $v(i)$ minus the mean in a neighborhood of i.

The window masks given here for the gradient and Laplacian operators are fairly standard, but many other operators have been defined, in many cases using larger windows, say 5 x 5. Also, notice that the gradient gives both magnitude and direction information about the change in pixel values at a point, whereas the Laplacian is a scalar giving only magnitude. This was only to follow the mathematical definitions and is not necessary. For example, a vector Laplacian can be defined whose x component is given by convolving the 1 x 3 mask $(-1 \quad 2 \quad -1)$ with the image, and whose y component is given by convolving the transposed 3 x 1 mask.

3.3   Smoothing Filters

Smoothing filters are designed to reduce the noise, detail, or "busyness" in an image. If multiple copies of the image are available or can be obtained, they can be averaged pixel by pixel to improve the signal to noise ratio. However, in most cases, only a single image is available. For this case, typical smoothing filters perform some form of moving window operation that may be a convolution or other local computation in the window. It is easy to smooth out an image, but the basic problem of smoothing filters is how to do this without blurring out the interesting features. For this reason, much emphasis in smoothing is on "edge-preserving smoothing", and many of the filters described below were designed for this reason. Typical filters are:

1.   Mean. The size and shape of the window over which the mean is computed can be selected. For a 3 x 3 window, the filter weights are:

	square window			plus shaped window		
	1/9	1/9	1/9		1/5	
	1/9	1/9	1/9	1/5	1/5	1/5
	1/9	1/9	1/9		1/5	

The square mean filter is separable. Let M be the 3 x 3 square window kernel above and let $m_v = m_h = (1/3 \ 1/3 \ 1/3)^T$ Then M is given by:

$$M = m_v \, m_h^T = \begin{pmatrix} 1/3 \\ 1/3 \\ 1/3 \end{pmatrix} (1/3 \ 1/3 \ 1/3)$$

2.   Weighted mean. A weighted mean is often used in which the weight for a pixel is related to its distance from the center point. For 3 x 3 windows, the weights may be:

square window				plus shaped window	
1/16	1/8	1/16		1/6	
1/8	1/4	1/8	1/6	1/3	1/6
1/16	1/8	1/16		1/6	

The square weighted mean window is also separable, with $w_v = w_h = (1/4 \ 1/2 \ 1/4)^T$.

3. Mode. A pixel is replaced by its most common neighbor. This is particularly useful in coded images such as classification maps (see chapter "Classification" on page 167) in which the pixel values represent object labels. Averaging labels makes no sense (what is the average of "rib" and "lung"?), but mode filters may clean up isolated points.

4. Median. A pixel value is replaced by the median of its neighbors. The median of a set of numbers is the value such that 50% are above and 50% are below. Conceptually simple, the median filter is somewhat awkward to implement because of the pixel value sorting required. However, it is one of the better edge preserving smoothing filters.

5. k nearest neighbor. Set $v(i, j)$ to the average of the k pixels in $n(i, j)$ whose values are closest to that of $v(i, j)$. A typical value of k is 6 when $n(i, j)$ is the 3 x 3 square window centered on (i, j). This is another filter used in edge preserving smoothing.

6. The Sigma filter [15]. Set $v(i, j)$ equal to the average of all pixels in its neighborhood whose value is within t counts of the value of $v(i, j)$. t is an adjustable parameter. This is called the Sigma filter because the parameter t may be derived from the sigma, or standard deviation, of the pixel value distribution. This filter is similar to the k nearest neighbor filter.

7. Filters based on pixel values and gradients.

Example 1: Inverse Gradient Filter [21]. Compute $v_{out}(i, j)$ as:

$$v_{out}(i, j) = \frac{1}{2}v_{in}(i, j) + \frac{1}{2}\left(\sum_{k,l \in n8} w(k,l)\, v_{in}(k,l)\right)$$

where the $w(k,l)$ are inversely proportional to $|v_{in}(i, j) - v_{in}(k,l)|$ and $n_8(i, j)$ is the neighborhood of eight pixels immediately surrounding (i, j). That is, neighboring pixels are included in the average with a weight inversely proportional to their pixel value difference (gradient) from the central pixel.

Example 2: Let p be the pixel at (i, j). For the gradient $|(x + x + x) - (y + y + y)|$ computed for the four sets of x and y shown:

```
xx     xxx     xx     y x
xpy     p      ypx    ypx
yy     yyy     yy     y x
```

set v_{out} to the average of the xs and ys with the minimum gradient.

Example 3: Compute a horizontal and vertical gradient (for example, the second and fourth gradients of the preceding example), and set $v_{out}(i, j)$ to the average of:

> $v(i,j)$
> $+$ $(v(i,j)$'s horizontal neighbors if the horizontal gradient is less than some threshold)
> $+$ $(v(i,j)$'s vertical neighbors if the vertical gradient is less than the threshold).

8. Maximum homogeneity filters. These are of the form:
   a. Determine the neighborhood of (i, j) most similar to v_{in}.
   b. Apply some smoothing using only points from this neighborhood.

The idea is to smooth within homogeneous areas, but not to include pixels from other populations in the smoothing.

Example 1: For the 5 neighborhoods surrounding the central pixel p given by:

$$
\begin{array}{ccccc}
xxx & xxx & xxp & xxx & xxx \\
xxx & xxx & xxx & xxx & xpx \\
xxp & pxx & xxx & xxp & xxx
\end{array}
$$

replace the value v_{in} of p with the neighborhood average closest to v_{in}.

Example 2: [17] For the 9 neighborhoods

$$
\begin{array}{ccccccccc}
xx & xxx & xx & xx & px & p & xp & xx & xxx \\
xxx & xxx & xxx & pxx & xxx & xxx & xxx & xxp & xpx \\
xp & p & px & xx & xx & xxx & xx & xx & xxx
\end{array}
$$

replace v_{in} with the average of the neighborhood whose standard deviation is minimum. (The neighborhoods include the central pixel p.)

9. Filters of the form:

> *If (some condition)*
> > *Apply filter method 1*
> *Else*
> > *Apply filter method 2*
> *Endif*

The objective is to perform one type of smoothing for noise pixels, and another for the others. A pixel is considered noise if it is significantly different from its neighbors. An example is:

> *If* $|v(i, j) - \overline{v(i, j)}| > threshold$
> > $v(i, j) = \overline{v(i, j)}$
> *Else*
> > *Leave $v(i, j)$ unchanged*
> *Endif*

10. Filters that fit a surface s through a neighborhood of (i, j) and replace v_{in} with $s(i, j)$. For $s(i, j) = k$, the surface is a horizontal plane, and the filter is equivalent to the mean filter. Including other terms in s such as $s(i, j) = s_0 + s_1 i + s_2 j$ fits tilted planes or higher order surfaces.

11. Closest of minimum and maximum [14]. A filter defined by computing the minimum and maximum in $n(i, j)$ and setting $v_{out}(i, j)$ to the one that is closest in value to $v_{in}(i, j)$ often produces good results by sharpening the boundaries between classes. The filter is typically iterated. It leaves isolated spikes which may need to be removed by another filter, say a medain filter, mixed into the iterations.

12. "Superspike." The superspike algorithm [18] performs a local averaging at each pixel, but uses the global image histogram to select the pixels to include in the averaging. Neighbors are included in the average only if (1) the neighbor's value is more probable than the central pixel based on the image histogram, and (2) there is no concavity in the histogram between the pixel's value and the neighbor's value. The idea is to favor the frequently occurring pixel values, assuming they represent the real objects in an image, and suppress the other values, assuming they are noise or boundary/transition pixels. The second condition is intended to include only pixels from the same category in the averaging. The algorithm is iterated, and tends to result in a histogram made up of a relative few sharp spikes.

Notice that some of the filters are defined to be iterated, and all of them can be iterated to further the smoothing. Some example results are shown in Figure 40, and a quantitative comparison of several of them is described in [12].

3.4 Edge Enhancement Filters and Edge Detection

Edge enhancement filters are the opposite of smoothing filters. Whereas smoothing filters are low pass filters, edge enhancement filters are high pass filters and their effect is to enhance or boost edges. The term "edge detector" is also used. This may mean a simple high

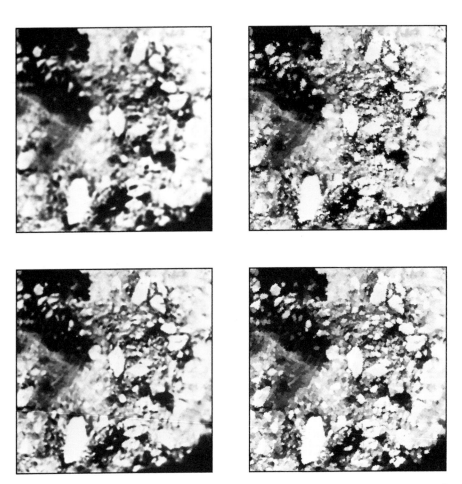

Figure 40. Comparison of smoothing filters: Clockwise from top left: 3 x 3 mean, 3 x 3 mode, 3 x 3 median, and maximum homogeneity (example 2 in text). The original image is in Figure 44 below.

pass filter, but sometimes may be more general, including a thresholding of the points into edge and non-edge categories, and even linking up of edge pixels into connected boundaries in the image.

Examples of edge enhancement filters are:

1. Gradient operators. A simple way of using them is to keep only the magnitude. Other methods keep both the magnitude and

angle. (We will see an example in chapter "Segmentation" on page 113.) The gradient in a given direction may also be computed. If the gradient at pixel p is considered as a vector (g_x, g_y), then the gradient in the direction of vector $d = (d_x, d_y)$ is $g \cdot d$.

Moving across an edge, the gradient will start at zero, increase to a maximum, and then decrease back to zero. This produces a broad edge. To identify only the central point as the edge, the output from the gradient operator is often thinned. An example of a thinning method is to keep only those gradient points that are a maximum in their direction. That is, let the gradient magnitude at a point be g_m and let the gradient direction, rounded to the closest of the 8 surrounding directions up, up-left, left, down-left, ..., be g_d. Then a point with a non-zero gradient is kept as an edge point only if g_m is greater than the gradient magnitude g_m. of the two neighboring pixels in directions $\pm g_d$. Otherwise, set g_m and g_d to zero.

2. Laplacian operators as described previously.
3. The Laplacian added back to the original image. Often a high pass filtered image is added back to the original image to boost edges yet maintain the underlying grey level information. This is illustrated in Figure 42. We say "added" to the original, but recall that the Laplacian operator we are using is the negative of the mathematical Laplacian, so we are actually subtracting it from the original to give:

$$v(i, j) - \nabla^2 v(i, j) \qquad \text{or} \qquad v(i, j) - \alpha \nabla^2 v(i, j)$$

where α is an adjustable parameter. For $\alpha = 1$, the 3 x 3 plus-shaped window Laplacian-plus-original looks like:

0	0	0			-1					-1	
0	1	0	+	-1	4	-1	=	-1	5	-1	
0	0	0			-1					-1	

and the 3 x 3 square window looks like:

0	0	0		-1	-1	-1		-1	-1	-1
0	1	0	+	-1	8	-1	=	-1	9	-1
0	0	0		-1	-1	-1		-1	-1	-1

Another way of looking at this filter is to say that it has the effect of sharpening edges by pushing a pixel away from its neighbors. To see this, consider that the above masks reduce to $(-1 \quad 3 \quad -1)$ in one dimension, and thus the filter may be written as:

$$v_i + (v_i - v_{i-1}) + (v_i - v_{i+1})$$

This is illustrated in Figure 41.

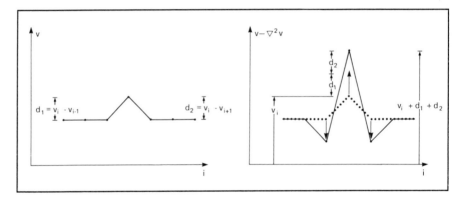

Figure 41.   The Laplacian as pushing a pixel away from its neighbors.

The Laplacian-plus-original filter is analogous to the photographic process of "unsharp masking". In this process, a film is exposed through a negative superimposed on a slightly defocused positive transparency, thus subtracting the local mean, and the result is an image with improved edges. Equation (3.5) in "Digital Approximations to the Gradient and Laplacian" on page 73 showed that the (negative) Laplacian of a function may be represented as the function minus its local mean. If the Laplacian is considered as $v(i, j) - v_l(i, j)$ where $v_l(i, j)$ is some low pass fil-

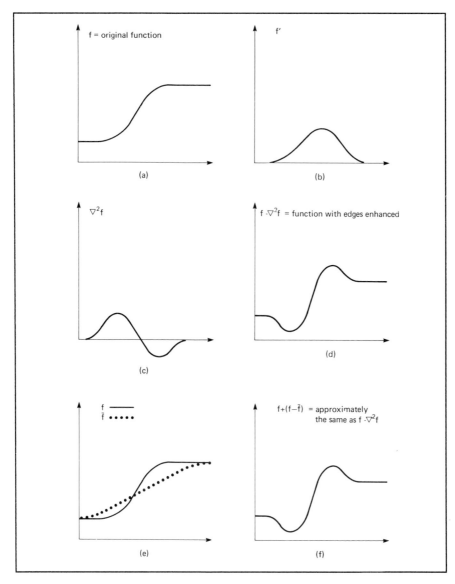

Figure 42.   Image sharpening: The first figures show plots of $f, f', f'' = \nabla^2 f$, and $f - \nabla^2 f$. Also shown are plots of f and $f + (f - \bar{f})$, which is a form of Unsharp Masking.

tered version of the image such as the local mean, then the image minus the Laplacian, scaled by α, is:

$$v(i, j) - \alpha \nabla^2 v(i, j) = v(i, j) + \alpha(v(i, j) - v_l(i, j))$$
$$= \beta v(i, j) - \alpha v_l(i, j) \qquad [3.6]$$

which, photographically, is unsharp masking. This is illustrated for a continuous function f in Figure 42(b).

In equation 3.6, the mean of the result is:

$$\overline{\beta v(i, j) - \alpha v_l(i, j)} = \beta \overline{v(i, j)} - \alpha \overline{v_l(i, j)}$$

and if the low pass filtered version has the same mean as the original, then this equals:

$$(\beta - \alpha) \overline{v(i, j)}$$

Therefore, $(\beta - \alpha)$ is often chosen to be 1, so that the mean of the result is unchanged.

Many variations of Unsharp Masking are possible by choosing the version of the low pass filtered image to use. Many of the smoothing filters described in the preceeding section such as the median, maximum homogeneity, and so on, have been used.

4. Marr operators [16]. These are the "Mexican hat" operators, and are filters of the form $\nabla^2 G$ where ∇^2 is the Laplacian and G is the two dimensional Gaussian distribution. The idea behind these filters is to first smooth the image with a Gaussian shaped filter, and then find the edges (using the Laplacian) in the smoothed image. These filters are often used on images that have noisy and slowly varying patterns such as those from medical and robotics applications. They can be defined for any scale, depending on the size of the edges to be detected. An example over an 11 x 11 window is:

0	0	0	-1	-1	-2	-1	-1	0	0	0
0	0	-2	-4	-8	-9	-8	-4	-2	0	0
0	-2	-7	-15	-22	-23	-22	-15	-7	-2	0
-1	-4	-15	-24	-14	-1	-14	-24	-15	-4	-1

-1	-8	-22	-14	52	103	52	-14	-22	-8	-1
-2	-9	-23	-1	103	178	103	-1	-23	-9	-2
-1	-8	-22	-14	52	103	52	-14	-22	-8	-1
-1	-4	-15	-24	-14	-1	-14	-24	-15	-4	-1
0	-2	-7	-15	-22	-23	-22	-15	-7	-2	0
0	0	-2	-4	-8	-9	-8	-4	-2	0	0
0	0	0	-1	-1	-2	-1	-1	0	0	0

5. Enhancement in direction of the gradient. An example of this type of filter is to compute the gradient at (i, j) and apply a one dimensional Laplacian operator in the direction of the gradient.

6. Just as for smoothing filters, high pass filters may be selectively applied. The filter:

$$If \ \nabla^2 v(i, \ j) < threshold$$
$$v(i, \ j) = v(i, \ j) + \alpha \nabla^2 v(i, \ j)$$
$$Else$$
$$v(i, \ j) = \overline{v(i, \ j)}$$
$$Endif$$

where α is a user-specified parameter, attempts to enhance edges (where ∇^2 is low) and suppress noise (where ∇^2 is high). $\overline{v(i, \ j)}$ is the mean in some neighborhood of $(i, \ j)$.

7. The previous operators are all fairly simple. More complex methods are also available. Much of the problem is in trying to work well in the presence of noise. If pixel averages are computed over non-overlapping adjacent square windows, a true edge should have different averages on either side for both large and small windows. A noise point may have a large difference for small windows but not for large, and a ramp may have large differences for large windows but not for small. Using this idea, a set of related methods proposed in [19] and [20] compute an edge at a pixel using products of differences of average pixel values in non-overlapping squares on either side of the pixel. Steps in the method are:

a. For each pixel in the image, compute $a_s(i, j)$, the average pixel value in the $(2s+1) \times (2s+1)$ square centered at (i, j).

b. Compute the four directional differences illustrated in Figure 43:

$$d_s^0(i, j) = |a_s(i, j+s) - a_s(i, j-s-1)|$$
$$d_s^{45}(i, j) = |a_s(i-s, j+s) - a_s(i+s+1, j-s-1)|$$
$$d_s^{90}(i, j) = |a_s(i-s, j) - a_s(i+s+1, j)|$$
$$d_s^{135}(i, j) = |a_s(i-s, j-s) - a_s(i+s+1, j+s+1)|$$

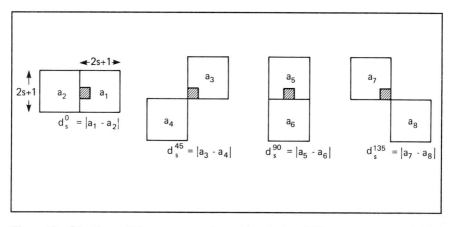

Figure 43. Directional differences computed around a pixel: Differences are computed using squares of side s for a range of values of s.

c. Repeat steps 1 and 2 for various values of s, say $s = 1,2,4,8$.

d. For each point and each of the four directions, compute the edge measure $E^d(i, j)$ as

$$E^d(i, j) = \prod_s a_s^d(i, j)$$

Then for each point, compute the edge measure as:

$$E(i, j) = \max_d (E^d(i, j))$$

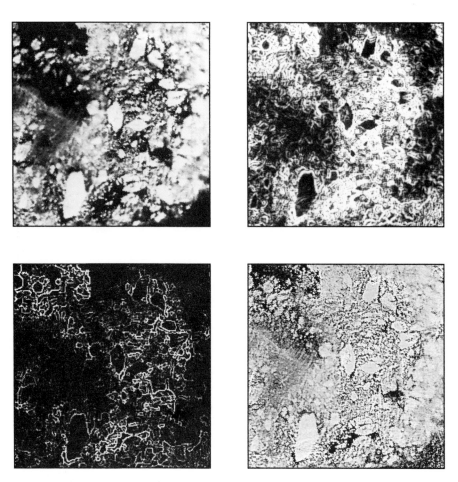

Figure 44. Comparison of high pass filtering methods : The original image (upper left), the magnitude of the gradient (upper right), the magnitude of the gradient thinned (lower left), and unsharp masking (lower right).

Although requiring more computation, this method is relatively immune to noise.

Some examples of high-pass filtered images are shown in Figure 44, and a quantitative comparison of certain of these filters is given in [19].

3.5 Discussion

The list of filters above for both low and high pass filtering is quite long, and many more are described in the literature. Even so, results from filtering operations are often rather disappointing. And though a filter may work reasonably well on one type of image, it is often not general. As an example, consider again the Superspike filter. A little thought shows that it will work well only on a specific type of image: one in which the noise pixels are close in value to their surrounding pixels (on the same histogram peak), and not equal in value to a large number of other pixels in the image. A noisy image of several blobs, the first with mostly value v_1, the second with mostly value v_2, and so forth, will be poorly smoothed. Noise pixels of value v_1 in blobs 2, 3, ..., of value v_2 in blobs 1, 3, 4, ..., and so on, will not be smoothed because they each occur on a separate histogram peak.

A more fundamental reason for the poor performance of many filters is that they are normally judged by a user against his own ability to visually filter an image, and this includes filtering, segmentation, interpolation, shape and object recognition, and so on. The simple filters described cannot approach this.

Often improvements can be gained, however, if the geometry, imaging conditions, or nature of the noise or features of interest are incorporated into the filter. For example, if the features are known to be horizontally or vertically oriented, or the noise is known to be multiplicative and not additive, then perhaps the filter can be modified. In this way, the filter masks listed in this chapter are only starting points for a filter which may be adapted to a problem. Such a case is shown in the chest X-ray in Figure 45(a). It contains a condition known as pneumothorax, which is the presence of gas in the space between the lung and the chest wall, and shows up as a faint, hardly visible line around the outer border of the lung. To help detect this edge, it was enhanced by applying a gradient-type of filter, but instead of using the standard gradient, it was rotated to always be approximately perpendicular to the pneumothorax edge [13]. For the top half of the image, the filter was defined as:

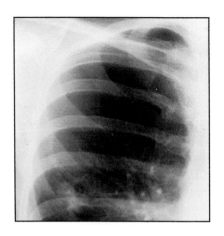

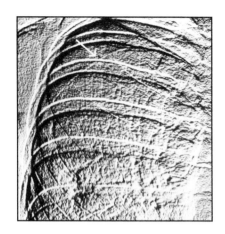

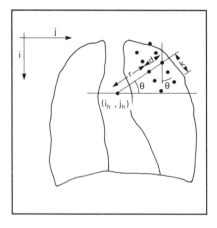

Figure 45. Adapting a filter to a problem: (a) The original x-ray in upper left. The edge to be found is known to follow the chest wall. (b) The output from the locally rotated gradient filter. (c) Diagram showing the parameters d, k, r and θ of the filter. The original image was provided by the Radiology Department, Brompton Hospital, London, and processed by Mike Cocklin, IBM Scientific Center, UK.

$$e(i, j) = \sum_{-n}^{n} v(i_h - (r + d) \sin \theta + k \cos \theta , \; j_h + (r + d) \cos \theta + k \sin \theta)$$

$$-v(i_h - r \sin \theta + k \cos \theta , \; j_h + r \cos \theta + k \sin \theta)$$

where d, k, r, and θ are as shown in Figure 45(c). k and d are user specified parameters controlling the size of the filter window. i_h and j_h are selected manually by a user and give the center of the circular shaped region made by the top of the lungs, the hilum in medical terms. The filter enhances edges perpendicular to the radial direction r. Results are shown in (b) with the pneumothorax marked by the arrow.

Apart from the advantage of adapting a filter to a specific problem, generalizations about the usefulness of the various filters are difficult. Of the smoothing filters mentioned, the median and k nearest neighbor filters perform reasonably well in many applications. Most high pass filtering is concerned with detecting edges, and gradient methods are usually superior to Laplacian methods because they are less sensitive to noise and they also provide directional information which may later be used to link edges and eliminate isolated edge points.

3.6   Questions and Problems

1. Compute the response of the Laplacian filter to the image patterns:

$$
\begin{array}{ccccc}
0 & 0 & 0 & 0 & 0 \\
0 & 0 & 0 & 0 & 0 \\
0 & 0 & 1 & 0 & 0 \\
0 & 0 & 0 & 0 & 0 \\
0 & 0 & 0 & 0 & 0
\end{array}
\qquad \text{and} \qquad
\begin{array}{ccccc}
0 & 0 & 1 & 1 & 1 \\
0 & 0 & 1 & 1 & 1 \\
0 & 0 & 1 & 1 & 1 \\
0 & 0 & 1 & 1 & 1 \\
0 & 0 & 1 & 1 & 1
\end{array}
$$

Does it respond more strongly to isolated points or to edges?

2. An image is smoothed with the 9 point 3 x 3 mean. It is still noisy and the output is smoothed again with the same filter. What smoothing filter will produce the same result in one step?

3. The edges in image I are detected by (1) applying the 5 point Laplacian giving image L and (2) thresholding L to keep those 10% with the highest values. However I is noisy, and L has too many noise edges. To avoid this problem, I is smoothed with the 9 point 3 x 3 averaging window, giving M, and the same two steps, Laplacian and thresholding, are applied to M. How does this image compare to L? (The purpose of this problem is to help demonstrate the nature and limitations of linear filters.)

4. For the signal:

$$0 \ 0 \ 0 \ 0 \ 30 \ 0 \ 0 \ 0 \ 0$$

will any of the following filters leave the spike unaffected? completely remove it? The mean, median, k nearest neighbor, sigma, and closest of minimum and maximum.

4.0 The Fourier Transform in Image Processing

The Fourier transform is a powerful tool for analysis and computation in many fields of mathematics and engineering. It has a wide variety of applications in image processing. In this chapter we present two of them: suboptimal image filtering and image pattern matching. We begin with a review of some definitions and properties of the Fourier transform.

Before starting, we comment on the term frequency. In image processing, we normally use this to refer to spatial frequency. Engineering students are often used to thinking of frequency as related to variations in time, but in this chapter, it is the frequency with which a signal (the image) varies as a function of spatial coordinates that is of interest. Images with gradually varying patterns have low spatial frequencies, and those with much detail and sharp edges have high spatial frequencies. It is this type of frequency that we are referring to when we speak of the frequency components of an image, and which we will compute using the Fourier transform.

4.1 Review of the Fourier Transform

The Fourier transform $F(\omega)$ of $f(x)$ is defined as:

$$F(\omega) = \int_{-\infty}^{+\infty} f(x)e^{-j2\pi\omega x}\,dx$$

for $j = \sqrt{-1}$. If f is periodic, F will be non-zero on a discrete set of values; otherwise F will be a continuous function of ω. If x is in units of spatial dimensions (e.g. meters), ω is in units of spatial frequency (e.g. meters^{-1}). There are limitations on the function $f(x)$ for its transform to exist: it must be a piecewise continuous function with left and right-hand derivatives at every point. However, the Fourier transform can be defined for certain "not-nice functions". We will not be concerned with these problems but will assume the transform exists for all cases we are interested in.

The inverse transform also exits, transforming $F(\omega)$ back to $f(x)$:

$$f(x) = \int_{-\infty}^{+\infty} F(\omega) e^{j2\pi\omega x} \, d\omega$$

Every f has a unique Fourier transform $F(\omega)$, every $F(\omega)$ has a unique inverse f, and we can transform back and forth from f to F. We use FT to denote the Fourier transform operator, and F to denote the transform. That is, $FT(f(x)) = F(\omega)$. Generally speaking we may think of $F(\omega)$ as giving the component of f at frequency ω. For example:

$$\text{if} \quad f(x) = \cos 2\pi\omega_0 x \quad \text{then} \quad F(\omega) = \begin{cases} \dfrac{1}{2} & \text{for } \omega = \pm \omega_0 \\ 0 & \text{elsewhere} \end{cases}$$

and if $G(\omega_0) = 0$ then $g(x)$ has no component of frequency $2\pi\omega_0$.

The Fourier transform is linear:

$$FT[\, af(x) + bg(x)] = aFT(f(x)) + bFT(g(x))$$

and has the scaling and shift properties given by:

$$FT(f(ax)) = \frac{1}{|a|} F\left(\frac{\omega}{a}\right)$$

$$FT(f(x - a)) = F(\omega) e^{-j2\pi\omega a}$$

If there exists an ω_0 such that $F(\omega) = 0$ for $|\omega| \geq \omega_0$, then f is said to be bandlimited at ω_0.

These definitions and properties may be extended to functions defined not on a continuous interval, say $(-a,a)$ or $(-\infty, +\infty)$, but on a discrete set of points x_i, $i = 1,2, \ldots , n$. The transform is then called the Discrete Fourier Transform. Both the continuous and the

96

discrete transform may be extended from one to two dimensions. The Discrete Fourier Transform in two dimensions is the form typically used in image processing, and means, in particular, that we may speak of the Fourier transform of a digital image. The definitions for the forward and inverse transforms for each of these cases are: (The three letters starting each line indicate Continuous/Discrete, 1 dimension or 2, and Forward or Inverse transform.)

C2F
$$F(\omega, v) = \int_{-\infty}^{+\infty} \int_{-\infty}^{+\infty} f(x,y)e^{-j2\pi(\omega x + vy)} \, dx \, dy$$

C2I
$$f(x,y) = \int_{-\infty}^{+\infty} \int_{-\infty}^{+\infty} F(\omega, v)e^{j2\pi(\omega x + vy)} \, d\omega \, dv$$

D1F
$$F(h) = \frac{1}{\sqrt{n}} \sum_{k=0}^{n-1} f(k)e^{-j2\pi hk/n} \qquad 0 \le h \le n-1$$

D1I
$$f(k) = \frac{1}{\sqrt{n}} \sum_{h=0}^{n-1} F(h)e^{j2\pi hk/n} \qquad 0 \le k \le n-1$$

D2F
$$F(h,i) = \frac{1}{n} \sum_{k=0}^{n-1} \sum_{l=0}^{n-1} f(k,l)e^{-j2\pi(kh+li)/n} \qquad 0 \le h,i \le n-1$$

D2I
$$f(k,l) = \frac{1}{n} \sum_{h=0}^{n-1} \sum_{i=0}^{n-1} F(h,i)e^{j2\pi(kh+li)/n} \qquad 0 \le k,l \le n-1$$

A property of the two dimensional Fourier transform is its separability. This may be expressed mathematically as:

$$F(\omega, v) = \int_{-\infty}^{+\infty} F_y(\omega, y)e^{-j2\pi vy} \, dy$$

where

$$F_y(\omega, y) = \int_{-\infty}^{+\infty} f(x,y) e^{-j2\pi\omega x} dx$$

This means that the two dimensional transform may be computed in two steps, first computing the one dimensional transforms for each value of x and then computing the one dimensional transforms of these results for each value of y.

A useful way of writing the equation for the discrete transform can be given by defining

$$z = e^{-j2\pi/n}$$

and then the matrix

$$Z = \frac{1}{\sqrt{n}} \begin{pmatrix} 1 & 1 & 1 & \cdots & 1 \\ 1 & z_2 & z_2^2 & & z^{(n-1)} \\ 1 & z_2^2 & z_4 & & z^{2(n-1)} \\ 1 & z_3 & z_6 & & z^{3(n-1)} \\ 1 & z^3 & z^6 & & z^{3(n-1)} \\ & & & & \\ 1 & z^{n-1} & z^{2(n-1)} & \cdots & z^{(n-1)(n-1)} \end{pmatrix}$$

That is, $Z(k,l) = z^{(k-1)(l-1)}$. Then the one dimensional discrete transforms may be expressed as:

$$F(h) = Z f(k) \quad \text{and} \quad f(k) = Z^T F(h)$$

and the two dimensional transform as:

$$F(h, i) = Z f(k, l) Z \quad \text{and} \quad f(k, l) = Z^{*T} F(h, i) Z^* \quad (5.1)$$

where $F(h)$ and $f(k)$ are vectors, and $F(h,i)$ and $f(k,l)$ are matrices. In this form, it can be seen that the direct computation of the one dimensional transform requires n^2 multiplies and the two dimensional requires n^4. Also, the separability of the transform can be seen: the two dimensional transform is equivalent to performing the one dimensional transform of all rows, and then performing the one dimensional transform of all columns of the result.

In the equations given, the discrete transform F is given for values of h (or for h and i in two dimensions) in the range $[0, n-1]$.

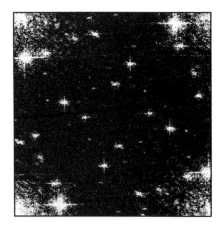

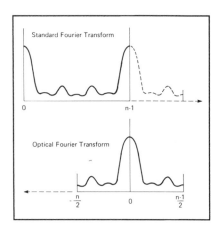
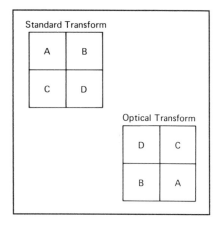

Figure 46. Comparison of standard and optical transforms: (a) The standard form of the Fourier transform in upper left, and (b) the transform rearranged into the optical form in upper right. (c), in lower left, shows the origin and coordinate systems for the two forms. The reordering to convert from one to the other in two dimensions is shown in (d).

For $h = 0$, the value of F is the constant or "dc" term. If the transform is displayed as an image, this constant term will be in the upper left corner, as in Figure 46(a). A more convenient way is to shift the transform to have the constant term in the center, Figure 46(b), and in this way it will match the more common presentation of the optical Fourier transform. These two forms of the transform, equivalent except for a reordering of terms, are referred to as the "standard" and "optical" forms. The reason for this shift is illustrated in one dimension in Figure 46(c), showing the coordinate system for the computed transform and that for the best display. Part (d) shows the shifting of the two dimensional tranform necessary to obtain the desired result. It can be shown that the result of this shifting can also be obtained by multiplying each pixel of the image to be transformed by $(-1)^{(i+j)}$ where i and j are the line and sample coordinates of the pixel.

Mathematically, the transform is defined for complex valued functions and the results are complex valued functions. Digital images are real valued arrays, say $n \times n$, but nevertheless the output has a real and complex part, each $n \times n$. However, the transform of a real function is symmetric, so not all the $2 \times n \times n$ resulting values are independent and there is no doubling of the amount of information. When displaying the transform of an image, such as the examples in Figure 46, what is displayed is $|F(h,i)|$, the magnitude of the complex number at each point. Because the "dc" or 0 frequency term is typically so much larger than all others, it is sometimes set to zero before scaling for display, or the logarithm of the values in the magnitude image is taken before scaling.

Several common Fourier transform pairs of one dimensional functions are shown in Figure 47. Figure 48 shows transform pairs of some two dimensional functions.

One of the most useful properties of the Fourier transform is known as the Convolution Theorem. It states that if F is the transform of f and H is the transform of h, then

$$FT(f*h) = FT(f)FT(H)$$

This may be written in several equivalent ways:

$$f*h = FT^{-1}(FT(f)FT(h))$$

or

$$G = F H \quad \text{for} \quad g = f*h \quad \text{and} \quad G = FT(g)$$

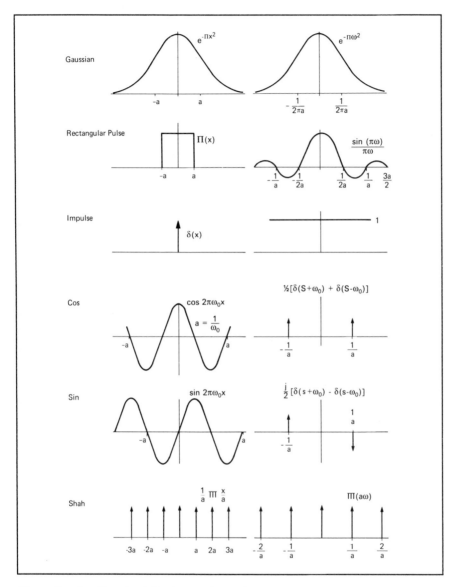

Figure 47.   One dimensional Fourier transform pairs.

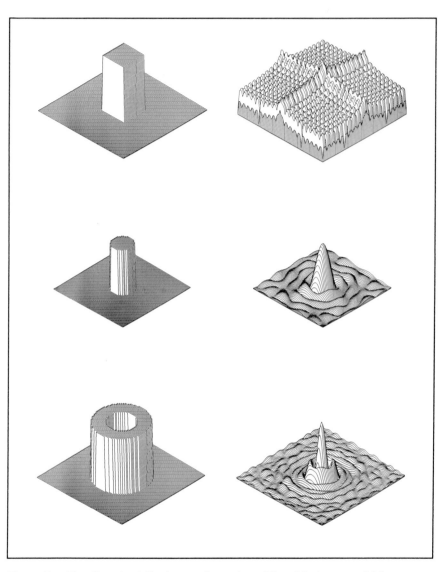

Figure 48. Two dimensional Fourier transform pairs: The original pattern of f for a square, a circle, and a ring, and the magnitude of the transform |F| are shown. For the circle and the ring, the transforms have been scaled horizontally, and for the square, log |F| is shown.

Thus convolution in the spatial domain is equivalent to multiplication in the frequency domain. This provides an alternative way of convolving two signals. Instead of directing convolving f and g, we may take their transforms, multiply the transforms point-by-point, and take the inverse transform of the result. The same is true for correlating two signals, which is a similar operation. (Appendix "Convolution and Correlation" on page 191 describes the relation between convolution and correlation.)

4.2   Fourier Image Filtering

The methods of Fourier analysis seem a natural choice for use in image filtering for two reasons. The first is computational efficiency. If a known, linear shift invariant filter $h(k,l)$ is to be applied to image $f(i, j)$, the output $g(i, j)$ may be generated as either a spatial convolution $f(i, j)*h(k,l)$, or, as described above, as $FT^{-1}(F\,H)$. There may be a large computational savings in using the Fourier transforms. The computational aspects will be discussed more in the next section on Fourier domain correlation.

Secondly, many imaging and optical systems can be analyzed using Fourier methods, and these naturally lead to filters that may be applied in the Fourier domain. Notice however, that the filter to be applied must be linear and independent of local image content. This was not the case for many of the adaptive, edge preserving filters of the previous chapter. This is the reason Fourier filtering is typically used to compensate for the effects of an imaging or optical system, whereas adaptive spatial filters are used when the filtering is based on pixel value, gradients, and so forth. As an example, a common problem for astronomy images is to convert an image taken by one telescope system into one compatible with an image taken by another. This is often most easily done by modelling the optics as a linear system using Fourier methods, and then applying the filter in the Fourier domain. And even if no model of the imaging system is derived, the Fourier transform can still be used to help select a (linear) filter. The two dimensional transform of an image identifies the spatial frequency components, and by eliminating or attenuating suspected noise components in the transform, then taking the inverse transform, a filtered image is obtained.

In any case, when using Fourier methods, H is specified directly in the frequency space, and the problem of filtering becomes one of choosing H. Roughly corresponding to the two cases of having a model of the imaging system or not, there are two general categories of filters: optimal and suboptimal. Optimal filters are those that are designed to maximize certain goodness criteria and use either the model, or measurements or assumptions on the signal and noise properties; for example, the shape of their spectrum. The Wiener filter and the Matched Detector are two categories of optimal filters derived using assumptions on the signal and/or noise. We do not cover optimal filters. There is extensive literature on their design and application in image processing. (See [1] for a good start.) These topics are normally considered as image reconstruction, and are different from the other methods described in this chapter, which are heuristic and qualitatively evaluated.

Suboptimal filters are those for which H is chosen by heuristic guidelines or by trial-and-error. Standard filters, such as Ideal and Butterworth filters, may be applied to suppress the low or high frequencies [2]. However, they may also produce artifacts in the filtered image. A common artifact is the "ringing" obtained in an ideal low pass filtered image. This can occur if high frequency terms are associated only with the noise in an image, and are completely eliminated. Ideal low pass filtering of simple geometric patterns in Figure 49 shows the effect. In the example of a digitized photograph, Figure 50, the same filtering produces a general motley and patchy pattern in the face. In both cases, the results are a natural effect of the cutting of all high frequencies which, although primarily noise, are also a valid component of the image.

Successful suboptimal filtering typically occurs when a specific frequency-dependent noise is to be removed from an image. An example is the noise coming from electrical signals in the imaging process and which can be visually observed in the image as periodic pattern. Another is the periodic noise induced in the digitization process of half-tone printed pictures in which the sampling frequency

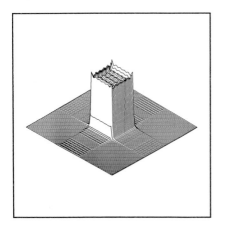

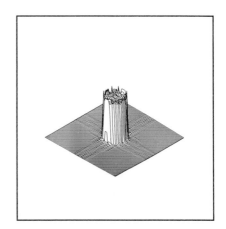

Figure 49. Ideal filtering of geometric patterns: These figures show the results of cutting all high frequency components. In the 256 x 256 transform, components outside the central 128 x 128 square were set to zero. The original images are those shown in Figure 48.

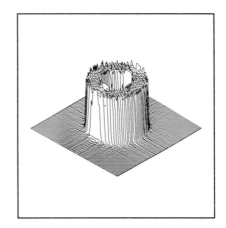

of the digitization interacts with the frequency of the printing matrix. In such cases, the noise component can often be observed as spikes in a display of $|F(h,i)|$. With appropriate software, the spikes can be outlined with a cursor, a filter constructed to attenuate those frequencies, and the filter applied. If the inverse transform can be computed rapidly, several filters can be tried to give a pleasing visual quality to the image. Figure 51(a) shows an example of this type of filtering. A periodic noise pattern due to the digitization process

Figure 50. *Ideal filtering of a digitized photograph producing ringing: Eliminating all high frequency components (the region of the transform shown in black) produces the ringing, seen in the face and neck.*

is visible in the transform shown in (b). A filter was selected by identifying the noise spikes interactively with a cursor, and the spikes were suppressed with a tapered rectangular window. The filter, shown as the black rectangles in (c), was applied to the real and imaginary parts of the transform, and the inverse taken. The result is shown in (d).

4.3   Fourier Domain Correlation

A second use of the Fourier transform in image processing is in performing correlations for pattern matching. Several applications arise in which it is desired to know where a (normally small) pattern image or window $W(i, j)$ best fits within another, larger array called the search area $S(k,l)$. (See, for example, the control point window and search area of Figure 65 on page 138 in chapter "Geometric Operations".) One way of selecting where it best fits is to pick the point of maximum correlation, illustrated in one dimension in Figure 52. Because of the Convolution Theorem, we may do the correlation in the spatial domain, as illustrated in the figure, or in the Fourier domain. The Fast Fourier Transform (FFT) is an efficient algorithm for computing Fourier transforms, and by using the

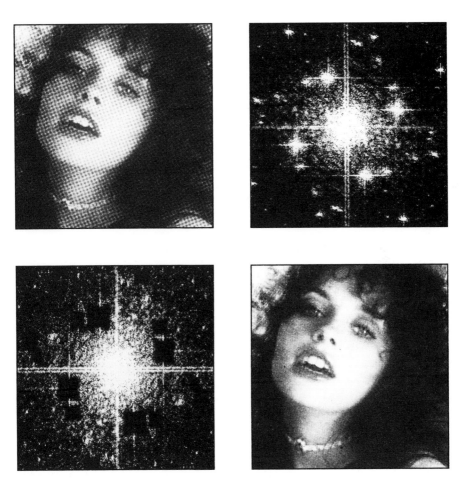

Figure 51. Fourier filtering applied to a digitized photograph : The frequencies to suppress were selected graphically. Nine rectangular windows (18 by symmetry) were defined to produce the output image, shown in lower right.

FFT, convolutions and correlations may often be computed more efficiently using the Fourier method than by direct spatial domain computations. Thus this use of the Fourier transform has no conceptual advantages but is strictly for computational efficiency.

To compare the computation times, suppose that we want to locate a $w \times w$ window W within a larger $s \times s$ search area S by corre-

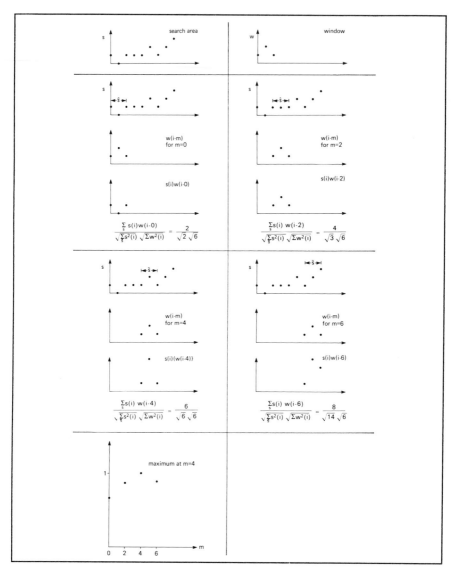

Figure 52. Correlation in one dimension: The window W is correlated with S by computing $\sum s(i-m)w(i)$ *and normalizing for each value of m. Only every other value of m is shown above.*

Using FFT:						γ is given by $s=2\gamma$
2d FFT of	w	lines	x	s	point FFT:	$w \times 2s\gamma$
window:	s	columns	x	s	point FFT:	$s \times 2s\gamma$
2d FFT of	s	lines	x	s	point FFT:	$s \times 2s\gamma$
search:	s	columns	x	s	point FFT:	$s \times 2s\gamma$
Multiply transforms:						$s \times s \times 4$
2d inverse	s	lines	x	s	point FFT:	$s \times 2s\gamma$
FFT:	s	columns	x	s	point FFT:	$s \times 2s\gamma$
Total Multiplies for FFT:						$5(2\gamma s^2) + 2\gamma ws + 4s^2$

Using Spatial Correlation:
Total Multiplies:
s-w+1 lines x s-w+1 columns x w lines x w columns

Ratio: $\dfrac{\text{FFT}}{\text{Direct}} = \dfrac{5(2\gamma s^2) + 2\gamma ws + 4s^2}{(s-w+1)^2 w^2}$

Figure 53. Comparison of multiplication operations using spatial and fourier correlation

lation. We assume s is a power of 2. For a direct spatial correlation, we must multiply each of the $w \times w$ values of the window with
the corresponding elements of S in each position of W within S. Using the Fourier method, we must take the two dimensional transforms of the search and of the window, multiply the transforms, and
take the inverse transform of this result. Using the FFT, a one dimensional s point transform requires $2s\gamma$ real multiplies, where
$\gamma = \log_2 s$ [22]. The number of multiplies required for both methods
is summarized in Figure 53. The most efficient method for a given
problem will depend on the specific sizes of the search and window
arrays, and whether the search size is a power of 2. As examples,
using the bottom line of the table, if we correlate a 20 x 20 window
in a 32 x 32 search area, the ratio of multiplies for the FFT method
to direct spatial correlation is about 0.86. If the same 20 x 20 area
is to be located in a 64 x 64 image, the ratio is about 0.33. Actual
performance comparisons of the two methods, which includes the ad-

ditions and other operations, have shown an even greater advantage for the FFT approach [23].

This advantage becomes still greater if the Fourier transform of the window need not be computed each time. This may be the case if the window is a fixed pattern whose transform may be pre-computed, or if it is a special pattern whose transform may be computed analytically.

In some cases, a normalization is necessary for results computed using the Fourier method. In the spatial domain correlations, the window is usually normalized to have zero mean and sum of squares equal to one:

$$\overline{W(i, j)} = 0 \quad \text{and} \quad \sum_{i, j} W(i, j)^2 = 1$$

and, at each position of the W array within $\check{S}$, the $w \times w$ elements of S are also normalized to have sum of squares equal to one:

$$\sum_{i, j} S(i, j)^2 = 1$$

where the sum is over the $w \times w$ array overlaid by W. This local normalization cannot be included in the Fourier correlation and if it is necessary, must be done as a later step.

As an example using Fourier correlation to find patterns, consider the astronomy image of Figure 54(a). Call this image A. To find the individual stars in A, they were modelled as radially symmetric Gaussians:

$$t(i, j) = e^{-\frac{r^2}{a^2}}$$

clipped to w lines by w samples. The transform of A was computed, the transform of the Gaussian model was computed, the two transforms multiplied, and the inverse transform taken. This was normalized by dividing each element by the standard deviation of the pixels in a $w \times w$ window centered on the corresponding location in A. Points of high values, corresponding to high correlations between the

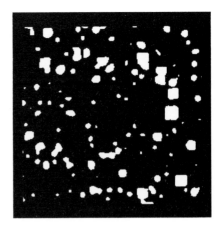

Figure 54. Locating features using correlation: Left: Original astronomy image of a star cluster. Right: Points of high correlation with a Gaussian star pattern for stars of radius 3.

Gaussian star model and A, were located by thresholding. The result for $a = \sqrt{3}$, an image indicating the presence of a star of radius 3, is shown in part (b).

4.4 Discussion

We have covered only two out of many applications of the Fourier transform in image processing. Other applications include its use in reconstruction (optimal) filtering referred to earlier, in image coding and compression, in image analysis and evaluation, and in computing shape descriptors for objects.

Whenever using Fourier methods, best results are obtained when physical considerations of the problem or image map well onto the Fourier model. This is often the case when deriving a linear filter describing an optical system such as a telescope or microscope. It is also the case when a periodic component or lattice is to be identified in an image. For this reason, Fourier methods are often used on images from astronomy, microbiology, images of a repetitive structure such as crystals, and so on. In other problems, this is not the case, and a Fourier solution may give poor results. For example, remote sensing images are usually not filtered with Fourier methods because there is no physical reason for suppressing or enhancing certain spatial frequencies and, for these images, the filters that are used are typically non-linear or the filter kernels are small and easily implemented as spatial convolutions.

4.5   Questions and Problems

1. What is the Fourier transform of the 9 point 3 x 3 mean window filter?
2. Compare the multiplications required for applying the 9 point 3 x 3 mean window to a 256 x 256 image in the spatial and Fourier domains.
3. Show that the matrix form of the 2 dimensional transform, equation (5.1), is equivalent to the 2 dimensional discrete Fourier transform equation DF2.
4. What is the Fourier transform of the triangle defined by

$$f(x) = \begin{cases} 1 + x & -1 \leq x \leq 0 \\ 1 - x & 0 < x \leq 1 \end{cases}$$

    (Hint: $f(x)$ is equal to the convolution of the rectangular pulse $\Pi(x)$ with what?)
5. The Fourier transform of an $n \times n$ image is an $n \times n$ complex valued array, or $2\,n \times n$ values. For reasons of symmetry, only $n \times n$ values are independent. Nevertheless, storing the Fourier transform of an image takes much more computer memory. Can you think of a reason why this is true?

5.0   Segmentation

Image segmentation is the process of dividing an image into meaningful regions. The simplest case is to have only two regions, an object region and a background region. Or there may be many object regions on the background, say many blood cells in a slide for a medical application. There may be many different types of regions. For example, in a natural scene to be segmented, there may be regions of sky, clouds, ground, building, and trees. In this case, the different categories are called classes. The segmentation process is not concerned with what the regions represent, but only with the process of partitioning the image.

Three general approaches to segmentation are considered in this chapter: thresholding, edge based methods, and relaxation.

5.1   Thresholding

Fixed thresholds. Single band thresholding is perhaps the simplest segmentation method. It assumes that the objects have pixel values generally different from the background. A binary output image, one containing only 0's (background) and 1's (object), may be created by applying a threshold:

$$v_{out}(i, j) = \begin{cases} 0 & if \ v_{in}(i, j) < threshold \\ 1 & otherwise \end{cases}$$

This can be extended to as many different classes as necessary by defining thresholds $t_1, t_2, t_3, ...$ such that:

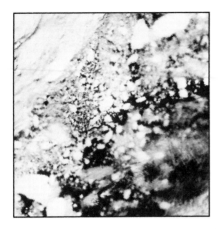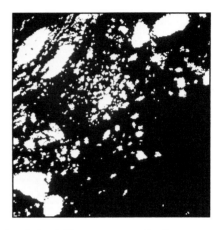

Figure 55. : *Results of applying a manually selected threshold to separate sea ice from water in a satellite image.*

$$v_{out}(i, j) = \begin{array}{ll} 0 & \text{if } 0 \le v_{in}(i, j) < t_1 \\ 1 & \text{if } t_1 \le v_{in}(i, j) < t_2 \\ 2 & \text{if } t_2 \le v_{in}(i, j) < t_3 \\ \cdot & \cdot \\ \cdot & \cdot \end{array}$$

The most common and reliable method of finding the thresholds is manual selection. The image is displayed, various thresholds are applied, and the best is selected by a user viewing the image. Figure 55 shows the result of a manual thresholding to segment a satellite image of a polar ocean area into categories of ice and non-ice.

Automatic or semi-automatic methods of finding the thresholds are available [26]. For example, thresholds may be defined between peaks in the one dimensional histogram. Because the histogram often has small fluctuations, some method of combining peaks is usually needed; for example, combine peaks that are close together, or combine peaks for which the ratio of the minimum between the peaks to the minimum of the two peaks is sufficiently small.

A similar method computes a histogram of the image excluding all points which have a large local gradient. The intent is to exclude edge points so that remaining points should be in uniform areas, thus giving better separation between histogram peaks. The thresholds are then defined at the valleys between the peaks.

Multiple and Variable Thresholds. In most cases, no single threshold is sufficient to separate objects from the background, and even using the manual method, a user must select among thresholds none of which gives all the objects without including extra noise or background. This is evident, for example, in Figure 55. Some alternative or additional processing must be done to obtain a cleaner result. One alternative is to use multiple thresholds or thresholds that vary across an image.

Assume that object pixels have a generally higher value than background pixels. Then two thresholds, t_1 and t_2, may be used by letting t_1 be the minimum value for object pixels and t_2 be the maximum value for background pixels, where $t_1 < t_2$. Pixels with value less than t_1 are background, greater than t_2 are object, and those in between are in the uncertain area. These are assigned to object or background depending on the assignment of the majority of their neighbors. This method must be iterated to resolve large areas of pixels with values between t_1 and t_2.

Another possibility is to vary the threshold across the image. The idea is illustrated for one dimension in Figure 56(a), where the threshold is varied based on the local pixel value mean. Part (b) shows two fixed and one variable threshold applied to an astronomy image to identify individual stars. The variable threshold was computed as:

$$t = k\sigma(i, j) + \overline{v(i, j)}$$

for $k = 0.18$. $\sigma(i, j)$ and $\overline{v(i, j)}$ are the standard deviation and mean in a neighborhood of (i, j). Such variable thresholding methods are closely related to the local pixel value mapping methods described in "Local Pixel Value Mappings" on page 45. There, the mapping applied to pixel values varied, whereas here the threshold to apply is varied. The same result can be obtained by applying a variable threshold to the original image as by applying a fixed threshold if the pixel values have been appropriately adjusted by a variable method.

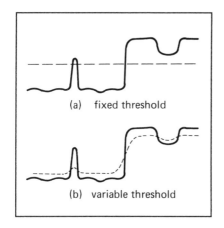 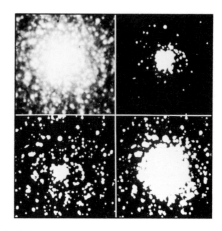

Figure 56. Variable thresholding: The idea is illustrated in one dimension on the left. Clockwise from top left for the image on the right: An original star cluster image with a varying background, a high global threshold identifying stars close to the cluster center; a low threshold identifying stars far from the center; and a variable threshold identifying stars throughout the image.

The methods described so far have been for thresholding a single band image. When extended to multiple bands, thresholding becomes a special case of image classification, which is considered in chapter "Classification" on page 167.

Shape Based Segment Smoothing. Thresholding methods often produce objects whose boundaries are irregular and jittery. Shrink/expand methods may be used to detect or eliminate these small irregularities, and thus provide a form of shape smoothing. The shrink/expand methods may be applied to any binary image, but they are described here because they are often applied to the output of thresholding operations. Figure 57 shows an object with two irregularities or "defects". Defect A, a convex defect, may be removed by shrinking the object and then expanding. The concave defect B may be removed by first expanding and then shrinking. To isolate the defects, the computed images may be subtracted from the original. Combined sequences such as shrink - expand - expand - shrink or expand - shrink - shrink - expand may be applied, but they do not produce the same result, as shown in part (b). The

116

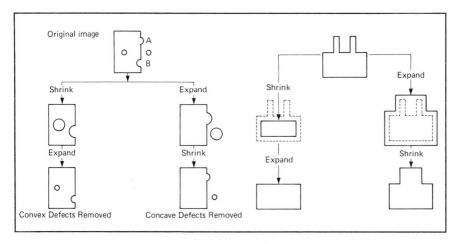

Figure 57. : Left: Illustration of shrink/expand and expand/shrink smoothing. Right: An example showing the order dependence of such smoothing methods.

shape smoothing resulting from a shrink/expand operation applied to the image of Figure 55 is shown in Figure 58.

5.2 Edge Based Methods

If edges are considered as boundaries between segments, it is reasonable to expect that by applying an edge detector, the boundaries between segments, and thus the segments in an image, may be detected. The problem is that edge detection methods just produce an edge measure at each point. Some method is needed of linking these into continuous and connected segment boundaries. Such a method [24] is described below. The steps in the method are:

1. Compute the gradient. Two new images, the edge magnitude and edge direction, are produced by applying a gradient operator as described in "Digital Approximations to the Gradient and Laplacian" on page 73.
2. Thin the edges. The gradient operator produces wide edges. The larger the window used for the gradient, the wider the edges in the magnitude and direction images. The idea of the thin-

117

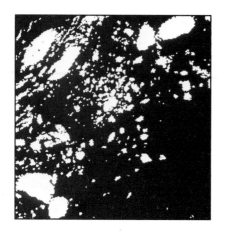 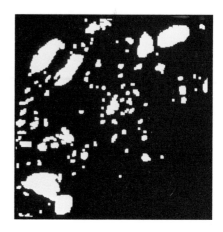

Figure 58. : Shrink/expand smoothing of a thresholded image. Input (left) and result.

ning is to keep only points whose gradient magnitude is a local maximum in its gradient direction. Referring to Figure 59(a), only the four directions labelled 1, 2, 3, and 4 are considered. Direction 6 is the same as direction 4, 7 the same as 3, and so on. The two neighbors in the direction that is closest to the direction of the gradient g_p of the center pixel p are checked, and if g_p is the largest, it is incremented by some constant and the other two are eliminated. (An alternative is to increment g_p by having it absorb a fraction of the value of the other two, and iterate the thinning.) For example, if the gradient direction is closest to direction 4, and if g_p is greater than or equal to g_4 and g_6, g_p is incremented and g_4 and g_6 are eliminated. The result is an image with (ideally) edges along object borders, but with only the one best point across the border at any point. See Figure 59(b).

3. Determine edge point neighbors. As a first step towards building up edge chains, each edge point is linked to two of its neighbors, called its forward neighbor and its backward neighbor. One or both of these may be null. Let g'_i be the vector orthogonal to the gradient g_i at i. Then g'_i points in the direction along the edge through i. Also let u_i be a unit vector from the center pixel p to its i-th neighbor. Possible forward neighbors f are those such that the vector dot product is positive:

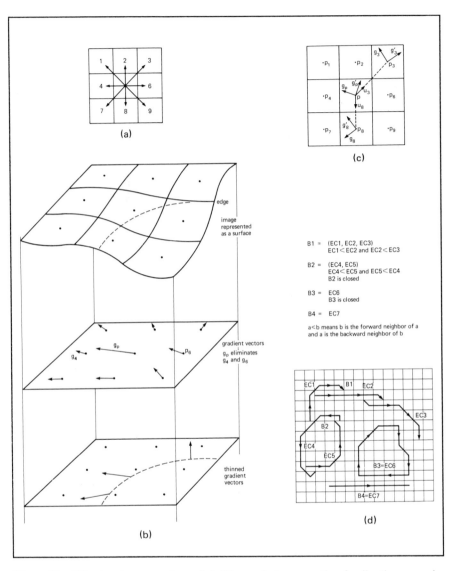

Figure 59. Edge based segmentation: (a) The numbering convention for directions around a pixel. (b) The results of thinning, leaving only one edge pixel at each point across a border. (c) Selecting forward and backward neighbors. (d) Linking edge chains into boundaries.

$$(g'_p + g'_f) \cdot u_f > 0$$

and possible backward neighbors b are those such that

$$(g'_p + g'_b) \cdot u_b < 0$$

These conditions require a consistent edge direction through p and f and through p and b, for example, high values on the left of the edge and low values on the right. Then f and b are selected as those non-adjacent neighbors that maximize:

$$(g'_p + g'_f) \cdot u_f - (g'_p + g'_b) \cdot u_b$$

See Figure 59(c). They are restricted to be non-adjacent to avoid sharply turning edges. Not all edge points will have forward neighbors and backward neighbors, corresponding to the extremeties of edge chains.

4. Link the edge points. With these forward and backward neighbors, edge chains may be defined as sets of edge pixels such that for each consecutive pair e_i and e_j, e_j is the forward neighbor of e_i and e_j is the backward neighbor of e_i.

5. Link the edge chains. The edge point linking will result in various types of edge chains as shown in Figure 59(d). These may be further linked into boundaries by joining edge chains EC_i and EC_j if EC_j is the forward neighbor of EC_i and EC_i is the backward neighbor of EC_j. See EC_1 and EC_2 in the figure. The forward neighbor of a chain is the chain containing the forward neighbor of the end pixel, and similarly for the backward neighbor. These linked edge chains become the boundaries of the image.

6. Extend remaining edge chains. Unclosed edge chains will still be common in the image, and to help close them, the unlinked endpoints of such chains may be extended a few pixels, which will cause some edge chains to close or connect to other chains. With these new connections, the edge chain linking of the previous step is repeated.

7. Eliminate edge chains. At this stage, an image consisting of a set of linked edge chains has been generated. Various methods

Figure 60. Results of edge based segmentation: The input image (left) and the output segmented image. The input image is simulated SPOT data, courtesy of GDTA, Toulouse, France, processed by L. Asfar and G. Savary, IBM Scientific Center, Paris.

may be applied to eliminate certain chains. Chains may be rejected if, for example, they are too short or too curvy. Other rejection criteria may be the average contrast along a chain, or a shape test such as the ratio of perimeter to area enclosed.

When these steps have been completed, a set of boundaries has been defined. Those that are closed define regions, and thus a segmentation of the image. Remaining boundaries are simply ignored. A sample result of the method applied to an image of simulated SPOT data is shown in Figure 60.

5.3 Relaxation

Segmentation by relaxation [4] is the name of a method that attempts to assign the pixels to segments in such a way that neighboring pixels are assigned in a "compatible" way. The method takes as input a set of probabilities that each pixel belongs to each possible class, and uses an iterative technique to update the probabilities. The updating is based on the possible segment assignments of the neighboring pixels, the associated probabilites of these assignments, and a measure of compatibility of the neighbors' class assignments and the central pixel's.

A key element of the method is a set of compatibility measures $c(k,s{:}l,t)$ that give the compability of assigning pixel k to class s and neighboring pixel l to class t. We will assume that $c(k,s{:}l,t)$ is in the range $(-1,+1)$ where -1 implies a strong incompatibility, $+1$ a strong compatibility, and 0 is neutral. Let $f^0(k,s)$ be an initial estimate of the probability that pixel k belongs to class s for all pixels k, and all classes s, and let n be the number of neighbors considered for each pixel, such as 4 or 8. To simplify the notation, only one subscript (the k or l in the formulas) is used to denote pixel location. Then a series of estimates $f^j(k,s)$ is computed iteratively as:

1. For each neighbor l of pixel k, compute the "neighbor compatibility" between ls possible class assignments and ks possible class assignments:

$$c'_l(k,s) = \sum_t c(k,s{:}l,t)f^{j-1}(l,t)$$

   where the summation is computed over all possible classes t.
2. Find the "average neighbor compatibility" for pixel k being assigned to class s:

$$a(k,s) = \left(\frac{1}{n}\right)\sum_l c'_l(k,s)$$

   The sum is over all neighbors l.
3. Repeat steps 1 and 2 to compute $a(k,s)$ for each class s.
4. Update the probabilities $f^{j+1}(k,s)$ as:

$$f^{j+1}(k,s) = \frac{f^j(k,s)(1 + a(k,s))}{\sum_s f^j(k,s)(1 + a(k,s))}$$

   for each class s.
5. Repeat steps 1 to 4 for all pixels k.

As the process is iterated, these probabilities tend to converge to certainty (0 or 1) so that pixels may be assigned to the class for which $f^j(k,s) = 1$.

The formulas given above for $c'_i(k,s)$, $a(k,s)$, and $f^{j+1}(k,s)$ were only stated, and not derived. Others are possible, and these were chosen to obey certain heuristic guidelines:

1. High compatibility pixels tend to reinforce each other and low compatibility pixels tend to discourage each other.
2. The degree of reinforcing or discouraging done by a neighbor is proportional to its own probability of assignment for each class.
3. The probabilities $f^j(k,s)$ remain in the range (0,1) and sum to 1. (The denominator of step (3) is a normalization just for this purpose.)

For a two segment problem, there is only $f(k,1)$ and $f(k,2)$ for each pixel k, and the mathematics simplifies because $f(k,2) = 1 - f(k,1)$. Another simplification is to set $c(k,1:l,2) = c(k,2:l,1)$. That is, the compatibility of class 1 being a neighbor of class 2 is the same as the compatibility of class 2 being a neighbor of class 1. Still another is to consider all neighbors equally so that $c(k,s:l,t) = c(s,t)$, which is reasonable in most cases. In this case the compatibilities reduce to the set: $c(1,1) =$ the compatibility of class 1 neighboring class 1; $c(1,2) = c(2,1) =$ the compatibility of class 1 neighboring class 2, equal to the compatibility of class 2 neighboring class 1; and $c(2,2) =$ the compatibility of class 2 neighboring class 2.

The value of these compatibilities may be derived from the joint probability density distributions of the classes. However a simpler method is to simply assign a positive constant to compatibilities for similar classes, and a negative number for different classes. When this is done, the relaxation algorithm will tend to assign groups of pixels with similar values to a segment and eliminate isolated points.

A result of the relaxation algorithm is shown in Figure 61. Part (a) shows the segmentation of an image before any iteration, assigning each pixel to the class for which it has the maximum probability, and parts (b) to (d) show the results after 1, 2, and 3 iterations. Eight classes were used, and the input probabilities were likelihoods

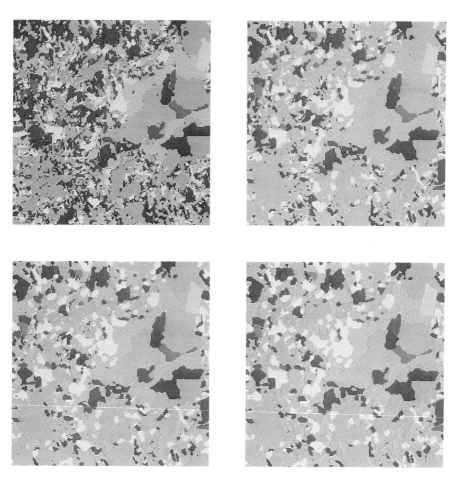

Figure 61. Relaxation: The initial image, upper left, has each pixel assigned to the class for which its probability of belonging is maximum. Results of relaxation after one (upper right), two (lower left), and three (lower right) iterations.

computed by a maximum likelihood classifier (see chapter "Classification" on page 167). The class shown in red was a mixed, uncertain class, and its self-compatibility was set low. The figure shows how it is eliminated by the other classes. Chapter "Classification" further discusses using relaxation for this type of problem.

5.4   Discussion

When compared to the results obtained by manual methods, the results of automatic segmentation are often poor. The methods described in this chapter are usually based on one or two properties, such as pixel value, gradient, or probabilities derived directly from pixel values, and these are typically computed over some small local area. On the other hand, a human can integrate shape, texture, orientation, edge, and grey level information at many different resolutions from local to global. Also, a human uses a scene model (a rib cannot appear in the head) and can extrapolate and interpolate patterns to resolve conflicts and fill in unclear areas. These factors belong to the field of pattern recognition or artificial intelligence, not just simple segmentation. Nevertheless, because they are not included, most segmentation methods are only one part of a larger process which must include checks on the objects identified, adjustments of thresholds, iterations, and so forth.

These remarks are similar to those made for image filtering, and although we have separated filtering and segmentation in two different chapters, they are closely related. A human observer never does just one, but visually filters an image to segment it, and segments an image to filter it. For digital processing, a well filtered image would be much easier to segment since there would be no noise pixels to induce false pixel values or gradients, and a well segmented image would be much easier to filter, by taking, for example, the mean of each segment. In fact, some of the filters, such as the maximum homogeneity filters, can be seen as attempts to locally segment the image and filter a pixel using only its neighbors from the same segment. In general, however, it has proven difficult to combine these two operations in a way that each can be used to improve the other.

As in the chapter on filtering, generalizations are difficult, but, of the methods presented, the manual based thresholding is certainly one of the most reliable when feasible (objects on a more-or-less fixed background and low throughput requirements), and the edge based segmentation has been successful in several different applications.

5.5 Questions and Problems

1. (Region growing.) Another class of segmentation algorithms uses region growing and region merging techniques. These have been less used than the other methods and one reason for this is an order-dependence that is often inherent in the algorithm. Apply a region growing to the small image below by starting with the upper left pixel as the beginning of a region and adding neighboring pixels to the region if their pixel value differs from the starting pixel by less than t. When a region is grown, find the next starting pixel by scanning row-wise from the upper left. Try $t = 1$ and $t = 2$. Now apply the same technique but start in the lower left. Use both $t = 1$ and $t = 2$. Are any of the four regions alike?

$$
\begin{array}{ccc}
1 & 1 & 1 \\
1 & 2 & 1 \\
4 & 2 & 4 \\
3 & 2 & 3 \\
3 & 3 & 3
\end{array}
$$

2. Give a geometric intrepretation for the terms in condition (1) of step 3 in the edge based segmentation method. Define another condition for finding the forward and backward neighbors.

3. Statistical Differencing (see "Local Pixel Value Mappings" on page 45) is used to adjust an image and a global threshold is applied. Give the equation for a variable threshold t which, applied to the original image, will give the same result.

4. The following image is input to a relaxation procedure:

$$
\begin{array}{ccccccccc}
0 & 0 & 0 & 0 & 0 & 0 & 0 & 0 & 0 \\
0 & 0 & 0 & 0 & 1 & 0 & 0 & 0 & 0 \\
0 & 0 & 0 & 1 & 1 & 1 & 0 & 0 & 0 \\
0 & 0 & 1 & 1 & 1 & 1 & 1 & 0 & 0 \\
0 & 0 & 0 & 1 & 1 & 1 & 0 & 0 & 0 \\
0 & 0 & 0 & 0 & 1 & 0 & 0 & 0 & 0 \\
0 & 0 & 0 & 0 & 0 & 0 & 0 & 0 & 0
\end{array}
$$

Pixels with value 0 have $f^0(0) = 0.6$ and $f^0(1) = 0.4$. Pixels with value 1 have $f^0(0) = 0.4$ and $f^0(1) = 0.6$. $c(0,1) = c(1,0) = -1$ and $c(0,0) = c(1,1) = 1$. Neighboring pixels used in the relaxation are the 8 immediately surrounding pixels. As the relaxation is applied, does the image tend toward a stable result.

5. Relaxation is used to segment an edge image. Initially each pixel is assigned $f^0(k,s)$ for 9 classes s. Class 0 is non-edge, class 1 is horizontal edge (0 degrees), class 2 is 45 degree edge, class 3 is 90 degree edge, and so on. In this case, is $c(k,s:l,t) = c(s,t)$? That is, is the compatibility of a neighbor's edge direction around a central pixel (assume it is an edge pixel) independent of the neighbor's position?

6.0 Geometric Operations

In this chapter we discuss geometric transformations of images. These transformations, or "rubber sheet" operations, include simple translations, rotations and scale changes, as well as warpings to remove highly irregular distortions such as those caused by perspective and view angle, irregular object plane, scanner motion during image acquisition, and so on. An example of a geometric warping is shown in Figure 62. An image of the San Francisco Bay area, taken by the LANDSAT MSS sensor, has been warped to lie on a digital elevation model, giving the effect of a three dimensional image.

The term registration is also used to describe geometric transformations. This emphasizes the fact that the generated image should register, or align, with some standard. For satellite images, the standard is often a map of the area covered by the image. Cartographers have defined various map projections such as Universal Transverse Mercator (UTM) and Polar Stereographic (PS), so the goal of satellite data registration is often to put the image into, say, a UTM projection. Another case is to register an image with another image of the same area taken by another satellite or by the same satellite on another date. In medical image processing, registration may be used to align two images of the same object. Two X-ray images, one before and one after the injection of a radio-opaque substance, may be registered to allow a pixel-by-pixel subtraction to remove background bone structure. In some cases, a full sequence of images from an X-ray motion picture may be registered to give a sequence, for example, of a beating heart. Registration of medical images is often done by simply shifting one image relative to the other. This works because the distortions between the images are small, and also because the images are, by the nature of the imaging techniques, blurred and with few sharp features to precisely align. On

Figure 62. Example geometric transformation: The input image (left) was transformed to lie on a model of the ground elevation to give the output image (right). (From a program by F. Ramirez, IBM Scientific Center, Madrid.)

the other hand, satellite images have both significant relative distortions and sharp, well-defined features, such as road intersections and other man-made objects. For this reason, much of the work to develop highly accurate registration methods has been done to register satellite images.

We call the image to be warped the input image, and the image we generate the corrected image or the output image. When the transformation is done to align the input image with another image, we call this other image the reference image. In all cases, two major steps are required to do the transformation. First the warping or deformation to apply is specified. This is normally done by specifying a mathematical deformation model defining the relation between the line and sample coordinates (i, j) in the output image and the line and sample coordinates (k, l) in the input image. Secondly, using the model, the output image is generated from the input image. The most common method of doing this second step is to resample the input image.

In the sections below, we describe the form the deformation model normally takes, how it may be computed using control points, how it may be efficiently applied using an interpolation grid, and then discuss methods of resampling.

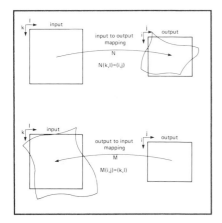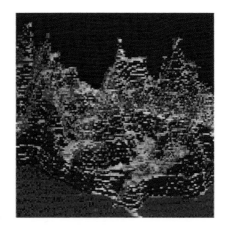

Figure 63.   : Left: Input-to-output mapping N maps input coordinates (k,l) to output coordinates (i,j).   Output-to-input mapping M maps (i,j) to (k,l).   Right: Detail from Figure 62 showing the black "holes" in the output image, resulting from the input-to-output mapping.

6.1   Deformation Models

Figure 63(a) shows an input image on the left and an output image on the right. Let us assume that deformation model N mapping from input coordinates to output coordinates is available. We represent this as $N(k,l) = (i, j)$. Such a model is called an input-to-output mapping.

It may seem that, using this mapping, the pixels of the input image may be "transferred" to the output image. That is, each input pixel location (k,l) can be mapped to location (i, j) in the output image given by $N(k,l)$. The value of the input pixel at (k,l) is assigned to the output pixel at (i, j) and the desired image obtained. This is the method used to generate the image shown in Figure 62, in which the input-to-output mapping N was defined by the matrix equation:

$$\begin{pmatrix} i \\ j \end{pmatrix} = \begin{pmatrix} i_0 \\ j_0 \end{pmatrix} + \begin{pmatrix} \cos\theta\cos\phi & \sin\phi \\ -\cos\theta\sin\phi & \cos\phi \end{pmatrix} \begin{pmatrix} (k-1)s_k z_k \\ (l-1)s_l z_l \end{pmatrix}$$

where

131

$$\begin{pmatrix} z_k \\ z_l \end{pmatrix} = z \times s_z \sin \theta \begin{pmatrix} \cos \phi \\ \sin \phi \end{pmatrix}$$

and

(i_0, j_0) = coordinates in the output image to which the upper left input pixel is mapped (a translation factor)
θ = zenith angle measured from vertical out of the input image plane to the viewer position
ϕ = azimuth angle measured from the input image k axis to the projection of the viewer's position into the input image plane
z = elevation at point (k,l)
s_z = z axis scaling factor
s_k = k axis scaling factor
s_l = l axis scaling factor

Part (b) of Figure 63 shows a blowup of a small portion of the output image of Figure 62, in which black "holes" may be detected. A hole results when there is an output pixel onto which no input pixel is mapped. This is a common problem using input-to-output mappings. It may also happen that several input pixels map onto a single output pixel. Either the last one is accepted, or some method of combining/weighting the input pixels must be determined. Another problem is that input pixels will be mapped to non-integer locations in the output, so a method of computing the value at the integer locations, that is, the output pixels themselves, must be determined. Usually the coordinates to which the input pixel is mapped are rounded to integer locations.

These problems occur with input-to-output mappings. An alternative is to use an output-to-input mapping. In Figure 63(a), transformation M is an output-to-input mapping that maps (i, j) to (k,l). If this mapping can be derived, the output image can be generated as follows. For each output pixel location (i, j), compute (k,l) by evaluating $M(i, j)$, giving the corresponding input image location and, at this location, pick up a pixel value, and assign it to the output pixel at (i, j). When a value has been assigned to all pixels (i, j), the output image is complete. The "picking up" is the resampling, which we come back to later. By using the output-to-input mapping, several problems of input-to-output mappings are avoided, and this is the method used most often.

A common case is for the mapping M to be a pair of polynomials Q and R in i and j:

$$Q(i,\ j) = q_0 + q_1\,i + q_2 j + q_3\,i^2 + q_4\,ij + q_5 j^2 + \cdots$$

$$R(i,\ j) = r_0 + r_1\,i + r_2 j + r_3\,i^2 + r_4\,ij + r_5 j^2 + \cdots$$

Then $k = Q(i,\ j)$ and $l = R(i,\ j)$. As an example, if $Q(i,\ j) = 0.5i$ and $R(i,\ j) = 0.25j$, the output image is magnified by a factor of 2 in the line direction and by a factor of 4 in the sample direction. Notice how the output-to-input mapping specifies the inverse transformation: $Q(i,\ j) = 0.5i$ expands by a factor of 2 since 0.5 is the inverse of 2.

We now consider ways of computing M. There are three general methods:

Scene/Sensor Model. The mapping may be computed using direct knowledge of the geometric warping to apply. For example, if a known scale change or rotation is to be applied, or a model of the geometric distortion produced by a camera or scanner system is known, the transformation may be derived analytically.

Direct Fit to Control Points. The mapping may be computed by fitting a function to control point locations. Control points are features located in the input image and whose location in the final output is known. If the registration is being done to force the input image to align with a reference image, the control points are features located both in the input and the reference images. This is frequently the case for satellite and medical images. For satellite data, another possibility is that the control points are located in the input image and on a map. In this case, the map coordinates (for example, latitude and longitude) may be converted to a line and sample coordinate system. The fit will produce a polynomial or other function causing the control points to be mapped from their locations in the output image to their locations in the input. All other points in the image will be mapped by the function, effectively interpolating between the control points.

Let (i_m, j_m), $m = 1,2,3, \ldots, n$ represent the line and sample coordinates of n control points in the reference (map or image), and let (k_m, l_m), $m = 1,2,3, \ldots, n$ be their coordinates in the input image. The coefficients of polynomials $Q(i, j)$ and $R(i, j)$ may be computed by the method of least squares. To do this, let Q be the vector of polynomial coefficients, let K be the vector of input image line coordinates, and let M be the matrix of monic polynomial terms formed from the output image line and sample coordinates:

$$Q = \begin{bmatrix} q_0 \\ q_1 \\ q_2 \\ \cdot \\ \cdot \\ \cdot \end{bmatrix} \quad K = \begin{bmatrix} k_1 \\ k_2 \\ \cdot \\ \cdot \\ k_n \end{bmatrix} \quad M = \begin{bmatrix} 1 & i_1 & j_1 & i_1^2 & i_1 j_1 & j_1^2 \\ 1 & i_2 & j_2 & i_2^2 & i_2 j_2 & j_2^2 \\ 1 & i_3 & j_3 & i_3^2 & i_3 j_3 & j_3^2 \\ \cdot & \cdot & \cdot & \cdot & \cdot & \cdot \\ 1 & i_n & j_n & i_n^2 & i_n j_n & j_n^2 \end{bmatrix} \cdots$$

The least squares solution for Q is, by definition, the one that minimizes

$$||MQ - K||^2$$

and is given by:

$$Q = (M^T M)^{-1} M^T K$$

A similar computation, replacing K by L produces R.

To do the fit, the number of control points must be greater than or equal to the number of coefficients in the polynomials. For example, a linear polynomial in i and j:

$$Q(i, j) = q_0 + q_1 i + q_2 j$$

of three coefficients, requires three control points as a mathematical minimum. Each control point gives two values, the i/k coordinate

134

and the j/l coordinate, so that only a total of three control points is required to fit two linear polynomials Q and R. However, because locating control points is often imprecise, it is best to have many extra points, say twice the number of control points as coefficients. If so, the effect of a few bad points is reduced.

Given Q and R, the line, pixel, and RSS (root sum of squares) residuals $r(m)$ of the fit are given by:

$$\Delta k_m = k_m - Q(i_m, j_m)$$
$$\Delta l_m = l_m - R(i_m, j_m)$$

$$r(m) = \sqrt{\Delta k_m^{\,2} + \Delta l_m^{\,2}} \qquad (6.1)$$

The residuals may be inspected to assess the overall quality of the fit and to identify erroneous points. Points with high residuals may be relocated or simply omitted from the fitting, so the process of computing the polynomials Q and R is typically iterative. By excluding or including points, relocating those with large residuals, or changing the degree of the polynomials, the user refines the polynomials to achieve a "good fit".

Combined Scene/Sensor Model and Control Points. The third and most accurate method of determining the deformation model uses a combination of control points and scene/sensor model. In this form, the model may include parameters such as the sensor position and pointing angles, and it is these parameters, not the coefficients of the direct polynomials, which are computed by the least squares fit. Figure 64 shows a set of mathematical spaces used in a model to correct LANDSAT MSS images. Beginning with the output image coordinates (i, j), a series of equations are applied mapping to the intermediate spaces of UTM, latitude and longitude, and then to a plane tangent to the earth at the point directly below the satellite, giving "actual" tangent plane coordinates. The input coordinates (k,l) are mapped through a series of sensor and viewing angle models to this same tangent plane, but in this case the coordinates are "observed" coordinates. The differences between the actual and observed coordinates are assumed to be due to the roll, pitch, yaw, and altitude deviation of the satellite as it gathered the image. A least

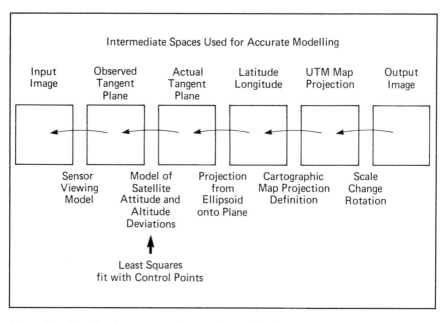

Figure 64. Mapping from output to input using model and control points: These spaces were used in an output-to-input model correcting LANDSAT MSS data.

squares fit is done using the differences to determine coefficients of roll, pitch, yaw, and altitude deviation models. With these coefficients, the complete mapping from output image to input image is available. With a sufficient number of control points to derive its coefficients, such a model can be very accurate, providing an output-to-input mapping with errors of less than, say 0.15 pixel. Of the three methods described, the combined scene/sensor model is the most accurate. It is also the most work, requiring a detailed model of the deformation, and these are not easy to derive. Thus this method is generally used only when high accuracies are necessary or in operational, high volume systems where the development effort is justified. The second method, a direct fit to control points, is often of sufficient accuracy and is widely used.

136

6.2 Control Points

If one of the methods above based on control points is to be used, the points must first be located in both the input image and in the reference. If the reference is a map or a digital image of significantly different scale or rotation, the points must normally be scaled by hand. However, in many cases, two images of approximately the same size and orientation are to be registered. In this case, there are three ways the control points may be found: manually, semi-automatically, or fully-automatically.

In the manual method, the points are located by a user in each image. A typical way of doing this is to display the images side-by-side or overlaid on a screen, and the user identifies the points in each image with a cursor, writing down the coordinates or having them read by software. In place of an interactive display, printouts and small scale photographic prints may be used. In the semi-automatic method, the user again identifies corresponding points in each of the two images, but here the location in one image is taken as the exact location around which a window is extracted. The location in the other image is taken as the center of a larger search area. The exact location of the control point in the search area is computed as the point of maximum correlation of the window within the search area. This will be described below. Here the user does not have to be as careful as in the manual method, and the process is quicker and easier. In the fully automatic method, windows from the reference scene are stored in a file or "library" and automatically located by correlation in search areas in the input image. The idea is illustrated in Figure 65(a) and a typical window and search area are shown in part (b). The estimated locations of the search areas must be computed, and for the automatic method to be feasible, there must be some way to do this with reasonable accuracy. For satellite image, initial estimates of ground features, given their latitude and longitude, can normally be made to within 10 to 20 pixels, sometimes much better, so this method is often used in operational systems for correcting satellite images. Typical window sizes range from 16 x 16 to 51 x 51. The size of the search area is chosen to

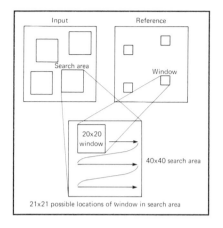

Figure 65. Window and search area arrays: (a) Automatic control point location using correlation. For fully automatic location, the windows would be extracted from the reference image and stored in a library. (b) On the right, an example of a window and corresponding search area.

guarantee that the feature is included and so depends on the uncertainty in the estimated feature location.

When doing the correlations for either the semi-automatic or fully automatic methods, let the window be of size l_w lines by s_w samples, and the search area of size l_s lines by s_s samples. Then there are $l_s - l_w + 1$ by $s_s - s_w + 1$ possible discrete locations at which the window may be overlaid within the search area. At each of these locations, the correlation coefficient $cc(k,l)$ is computed as:

$$cc(k,l) = \frac{\displaystyle\sum_{i=1}^{l_w}\sum_{j=1}^{s_w}(w_{i,j} - \overline{w})(s_{k-1+i,l-1+j} - \overline{s}_{k,l})}{\sqrt{\displaystyle\sum_{i=1}^{l_w}\sum_{j=1}^{s_w}(w_{i,j} - \overline{w})^2}\sqrt{\displaystyle\sum_{i=1}^{l_w}\sum_{j=1}^{s_w}(s_{k-1+i,l-1+j} - \overline{s}_{k,l})^2}} \quad (6.2)$$

giving the array $cc(k,l)$ for $k = 1,2,...l_s - l_w + 1$, $l = 1,2,...s_s - s_w + 1$. $\overline{s}_{k,l}$ is the mean of the $l_w \times s_w$ portion of the search area centered on (k,l). The point giving the maximum correlation is taken as the location of the window within the search area.

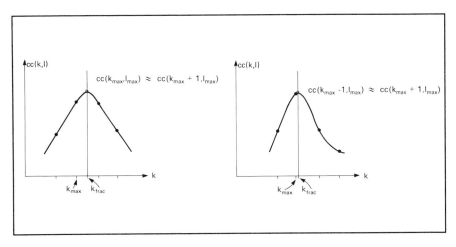

Figure 66. : Interpolating to sub-pixel locations based on correlation values computed at integer locations. The two cases shown are: $cc(k_{max}, l_{max}) \cong cc(k_{max}+1, l_{max})$ and $cc(k_{max}-1, l_{max}) \cong cc(k_{max}+1, l_{max})$.

For high geometric accuracies, the control point coordinates found by correlation may be interpolated to sub-pixel (fractional) levels. For example, let (k_{max}, l_{max}) be the indices of $cc(k,l)$ giving its maximum value. Then one form of interpolation is:

$$k_{frac} = (k_{max} - \frac{1}{2}) +$$

$$\frac{cc(k_{max}, l_{max}) - cc(k_{max}-1, l_{max})}{cc(k_{max}, l_{max}) - cc(k_{max}-1, l_{max}) + cc(k_{max}, l_{max}) - cc(k_{max}+1, l_{max})}$$

and

$$l_{frac} = (k_{max} - \frac{1}{2}) +$$

$$\frac{cc(k_{max}, l_{max}) - cc(k_{max}, l_{max}-1)}{cc(k_{max}, l_{max}) - cc(k_{max}, l_{max}-1) + cc(k_{max}, l_{max}) - cc(k_{max}, l_{max}+1)}$$

This interpolation has the properties, shown in Figure 66, that:

If $cc(k_{max}, l_{max}) \cong cc(k_{max}+1, l_{max})$ then $k_{frac} \cong k_{max} + \frac{1}{2}$

and

If $cc(k_{max} -1, l_{max}) \cong cc(k_{max} +1, l_{max})$ then $k_{frac} \cong k_{max}$

Another method of interpolating to subpixel values is to fit a continuous two-dimensional surface $s(k,l)$ to the $cc(k,l)$ matrix in the vicinity of the maximum and find the maximum of the surface. This requires a numerical technique to find the maximum of the two dimensional surface.

Section "Review of the Fourier Transform" on page 95 discussed using the Fourier transform to perform image correlations of the type given by equation 6.2. (See Appendix "Convolution and Correlation" on page 191 for the relation between convolution and correlation.) As mentioned in that section, the advantages of the Fourier approach depend on the sizes of the search and window arrays. Because the window array is smaller than the search area, it must be padded, say with zeroes, to the size of the search area. Then the two arrays are the same size, their transforms are the same size, and they may be multiplied together. Taking the inverse transform of the product gives the correlation matrix $cc(k,l)$, although in this case it is of size $l_s \, x \, s_s$, not $(l_s - l_w + 1) \, x \, (s_s - s_w + 1)$. The extra values are uninteresting, being locations where part of the window is wrapped around on the search area; for example, the window starts near the right edge of the search area, and a part of it is wrapped back onto the left.

In using equation (6.2) for spatial correlation, the subimage of the search area which the window overlays at each possible position is normalized as part of the computation. This is the second term in the denominator. When doing the correlation using the Fourier method, the entire search area is normalized, not each window position, so results are not identical. But this is not normally a problem. Both spatial and frequency domain correlation are widely used to perform control point correlations.

6.3   Interpolation Grids

We now have considered ways of computing the output-to-input deformation model, and ways of finding control points when they are necessary. Let us assume that these have been done and the model M is available. It may be a pair of polynomials or a detailed scene and sensor model. In any case, it maps points (i, j) in the output image to (k,l) in the input image.

The mapping may be computationally expensive to apply. Scene/sensor models may be quite complex, involving long sequences of equations and iterative steps. Even high order polynomials are expensive if we are speaking of mapping every pixel in an image. As a whole, the derivatives of the model with respect to i and j are almost always quite small, and they can be approximated locally by linear functions. Thus a standard technique is to define a grid on the output image and map only the grid points by M. All other points are found by bilinear interpolation within the grid as shown in Figure 67. This mapping is much less expensive, and for suitably spaced grid points, the loss of accuracy is negligible, say 0.01 pixels. For these reasons, interpolation grids are widely used to perform the output-to-input mappings. The spacing of the grid depends on the order of the deformation model, but as an example, a grid giving one grid point about every 80 input pixels is easily sufficient for LANDSAT MSS data.

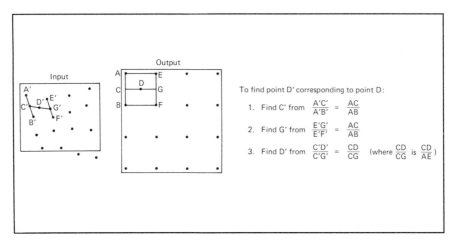

Figure 67. An interpolation grid in the output and input images: For an output-to-input mapping (the case shown), the grid is regular in the output image.

6.4 Resampling

We can now efficiently map pixel locations from the output image to the input image, and we are ready to consider the "picking up" of a pixel value we mentioned earlier. This is resampling, and we begin our discussion in one dimension.

Interpolating a Digital Signal. Sampling a continuous one-dimensional signal $f(x)$ is the process of selecting a discrete set of points $f(x_1), f(x_2), f(x_3), ...$ from the signal. To reconstruct the complete signal from the sampled values, a form of interpolation between the samples is used. This interpolation is called resampling. Resampling is in fact a general term and means to convert a sampled signal into another sampled signal that represents the original continuous signal as it would appear sampled with different sampling parameters. The linear filtering operations described in chapter "Filtering" on page 69 are a form of resampling in which parameters of the impulse response of the sampling system were changed but the geometry of the image was left alone. In geometric resampling, it will be the geometric parameters, the spacing and orientation, which are primarily of interest. However, we will see that even in a geometric resampling, the parameters of the impulse response are affected.

Consider an example. Suppose we have a digitized image $v(i, j)$ for $i = 1,...,256$ and $j = 1,...,256$, and we want to display this on a screen of size 512 x 512, using all points of the screen. (In terms of our previous discussion, we can think of this as having the mapping polynomials $Q(i, j) = 0.5i$ and $R(i, j) = 0.5j$.) Additional pixels are required. Each pixel in each line could be repeated, and each line repeated to give the required number of pixels. However, if we think of $v(i, j)$ as samples of some known continuous signal $V(x,y)$, we could evaluate V at the intermediate points $i,j = 1.5, 2.5, 3.5,...$ to obtain the additional points. This becomes even more desirable if we think of the original image as having pixels at $i = 1,2,...,174, j = 1,2,3,...415$ for example, and wanting to display the image on the same 512 x 512 screen. There is no simple pixel duplication that will give the required number of pixels. A general interpolation method is needed.

Going back to one dimension, the problem is illustrated in Figure 68 where we need to find a value for $f(x)$ for any x. This problem is often referred to as that of "reconstructing" f. Although f is not reconstructed in the sense that a closed formula, for example, a polynomial or trigonometric function, is derived, it is reconstructed in the sense that an expression is derived giving f at any point x in terms of the points in some neighborhood of x.

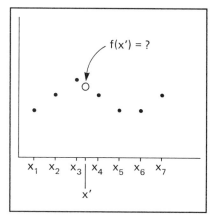

Figure 68. : Illustration of a sampled one-dimensional signal and the need to interpolate to reconstruct intermediate values.

The simplest method of assigning a value to $f(x)$ is to take $f(x_i)$ for the x_i closest to x. This is called nearest neighbor (NN) resampling or zero order interpolation. Another method is to linearly interpolate between x_i and x_{i+1} where $x_i \leq x < x_{i+1}$. This is linear interpolation and when extended to two dimensions is called bilinear interpolation. It is first order interpolation. (Note: This bilinear interpolation should not be confused with the bilinear interpolation done using the grid points to speed up the output-to-input mapping. That bilinear interpolation maps an output point to the input. The one described here computes a pixel's value.) Higher order interpolation involves fitting some curve to the $f(x_i)$ for the x_i in some neighborhood of x, and evaluating the curve at x. To specify an interpolation method, the form of the curve could be given, but an equivalent and more common method is to specify the weighting function $h(s)$ of the method. The function $h(s)$ gives the weight to assign to neighboring pixels as a function of their distance s from x in order to interpolate at the point x. Then:

$$f(x) = \sum f(x_i)\, h(x_i - x) \tag{6.3}$$

Cubic convolution [31] is the name of an interpolation method using two cubic polynomials to define the weighting coefficients for the four surrounding points, two to the left and two to the right. The interpolating curves and weighting functions for nearest neighbor, bilinear interpolation, and cubic convolution, are shown below and illustrated in Figure 69. The interpolating curves are derived from the weighting functions by equation (6.3) above.

Nearest neighbor:

$$f(x) = f(x_i) \quad \text{for the } x_i \text{ closest to } x$$

$$h_{NN}(x) = \begin{cases} 1 & -\dfrac{1}{2} \le x < \dfrac{1}{2} \\ 0 & \textit{otherwise} \end{cases}$$

Linear interpolation (bilinear in two dimensions):

$$f(x) = bi(f(x_i), f(x_{i+1}), d)$$

for
$$bi(y_1, y_2, d) = y_1(1 - d) + y_2 d$$

$$h_{BI}(x) = \begin{cases} 1 - x & 0 \le x < 1 \\ 0 & x \ge 1 \\ h(-x) & x < 0 \end{cases}$$

Cubic convolution:

$$f(x) = cc(f(x_{i-1}),\ f(x_i),\ f(x_{i+1}),\ f(x_{i+2}), d)$$

for
$$cc(y_1,\ y_2,\ y_3,\ y_4,\ d) =$$
$$y_2 + d((-y_1 + y_3) + d((2y_1 - 2y_2 + y_3 - y_4) + d(-y_1 + y_2 - y_3 + y_4)))$$

144

$$h_{CC}(x) = \begin{cases} 1 - 2x^2 + x^3 & 0 \le x < 1 \\ 4 - 8x + 5x^2 - x^3 & 1 \le x < 2 \\ 0 & x > 2 \\ h(-x) & x < 0 \end{cases}$$

For both *bi* and *cc*, i is such that $x_i \le x < x_{i+1}$ and $d = x - x_i$.

Fourier Analysis of Sampling and Interpolation. The Fourier transform provides a means of analyzing the effects of sampling a continuous signal and of reconstructing a continuous signal from a sampled one, and it allows us to answer such questions as:

1. Given that we have a continuous signal, how densely should we sample it so that later we can accurately reconstruct it from the samples?
2. Given that we have a sampled signal, what is the best method of interpolating to do the resampling? What assumptions must we place on the original sampling and the original signal?

We give the results only in graphical form. Figure 70 shows the sampling and reconstruction process in both the spatial and frequency (Fourier) domains. The top of the figure shows a continuous bandlimited function f and its transform, with ω_0 the cutoff frequency. Recall that a bandlimited signal f is one for which there exists a ω_0 such that the transform F of f has no component at frequency ω for $|\omega| \ge \omega_0$. The large but finite window d has a narrow spike, almost a delta function, as its transform D, and applying the window to f has little effect on the transform, which is $D*F$. We will assume an infinite window so D is a spike and $D*F = F$. The sampling function s has transform S, and produces $S*D*F$. To isolate the central copy of F in $S*D*F$, the frequency domain square window I is applied giving $I(S*D*F)$. This corresponds to spatial domain convolution with function i. In Figure 47, the transform of a square window is listed as the sinc function:

$$sinc(x) = \frac{\sin(\pi x)}{\pi x}$$

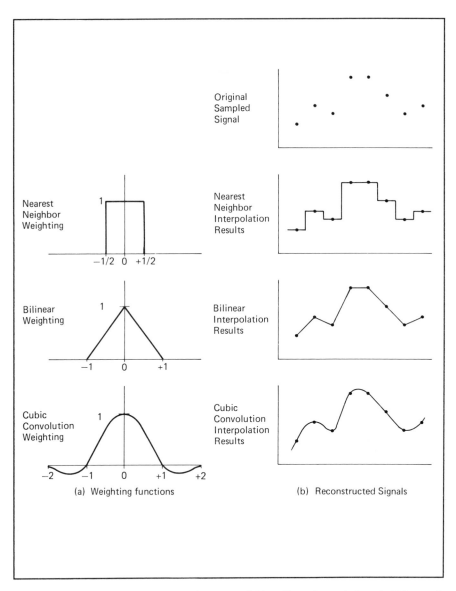

Original
Sampled
Signal

Nearest
Neighbor
Weighting

1

−1/2 0 +1/2

Nearest
Neighbor
Interpolation
Results

Bilinear
Weighting

1

−1   0   +1

Bilinear
Interpolation
Results

Cubic
Convolution
Weighting

1

−2   −1   0   +1   +2

Cubic
Convolution
Interpolation
Results

(a) Weighting functions

(b) Reconstructed Signals

Figure 69. : Graphical comparison of nearest neighbor, linear interpolation, (which extends to bilinear in two dimensions), and cubic convolution.

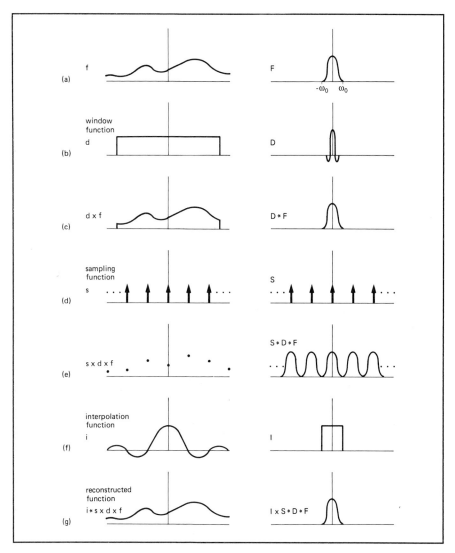

Figure 70. : *Graphical representation of sampling and resampling in the spatial and frequency domains. From top to bottom: the original signal, the finite window and its application to the signal, the sampling function and its application, and the interpolating function and its application, reproducing the original signal. The important result is that, with appropriate assumptions, sinc(x) is the ideal interpolation function to reconstruct a sampled signal.*

Applying the square window I in the frequency domain, we have that $I(S*D*F)$ is equal to F. From this it follows that $i*s\,df$ is equal to f, so that we have reconstructed the original signal from the sampled signal. The operation can be summarized by saying that if (1) f is band limited at ω_0 and (2) f is sampled with spacing less than or equal to $1/(2\,\omega_0)$, then f can be reconstructed by convolving the samples with the sinc function. The reconstructed signal f is given at any point x by:

$$f(x) = \sum f(x_i)2\omega_0 sinc(2\omega_0(x - x_i))$$

Although, strictly speaking, this equation cannot be implemented on a computer because it contains an infinite sum, the $sinc(x)$ weighting terms drop off rapidly enough so that only a few terms are necessary for good approximations. The cubic convolution interpolation mentioned earlier is actually an approximation to sinc. Using only four terms, it produces excellent results.[3]

Resampling for Geometric Transformations. Returning now to our main discussion of geometric transformations, we have all the necessary steps, and the output image may be generated by computing a value for each output pixel (i, j), $i = 1,...,nl$ and $j = 1,...,ns$ as follows:

1. Map (i, j) to the input image using bilinear interpolation on the grid to produce (k,l). Although (i, j) is an integer location, in general (k,l) is fractional.

2. If point (k,l) falls outside the input image (k is less than 1 or greater than the number of lines, or l is less than 1 or greater than the number of samples) set pixel value v to a fill character, say black.

---

[3]

Cubic convolution is actually a family of interpolation methods all of which approximate $sinc(x)$. The most common form is the one given on page 144, but others may be derived using different conditions in the approximation. See Problem 1 at the end of this chapter.

3. Otherwise at point (k,l), perform a resampling such as nearest neighbor, bilinear interpolation, or cubic convolution to produce v. In two dimensions, these may be written as:

Nearest Neighbor.

$$v = v_{in}(k', l')$$

where (k', l') is the input image location closest to (k,l).

Bilinear Interpolation.

$$t_1 = bi(v_{in}(K, L), v_{in}(K+1,L),c)$$
$$t_2 = bi(v_{in}(K, L+1), v_{in}(K+1,L+1),c)$$
$$v = bi(t_1,t_2, d)$$

Cubic Convolution.

$$t_1 = cc(v_{in}(K-1,L-1), v_{in}(K-1,L), v_{in}(K-1,L+1), v_{in}(K-1,L+2), c)$$
$$t_2 = cc(v_{in}(K,L-1), v_{in}(K,L), v_{in}(K,L+1), v_{in}(K,L+2), c)$$
$$t_3 = cc(v_{in}(K+1,L-1), v_{in}(K+1,L), v_{in}(K+1,L+1), v_{in}(K+1,L+2), c)$$
$$t_4 = cc(v_{in}(K+2,L-1), v_{in}(K+2,L), v_{in}(K+2,L+1), v_{in}(K+2,L+2), c)$$
$$v = cc(t_1, t_2, t_3, t_4, d)$$

where

$$K = \text{the integer part of } k$$
$$L = \text{the integer part of } l$$
$$c = k - K$$
$$d = l - L$$

and *bi* and *cc* are the bilinear and cubic convolution interpolation functions defined on page 144.

4. Assign the output pixel at (i, j) the value v.

The result is the corrected image.

An example of a geometric transformation is shown in Figure 71, and the effects of the different interpolation methods can be seen.

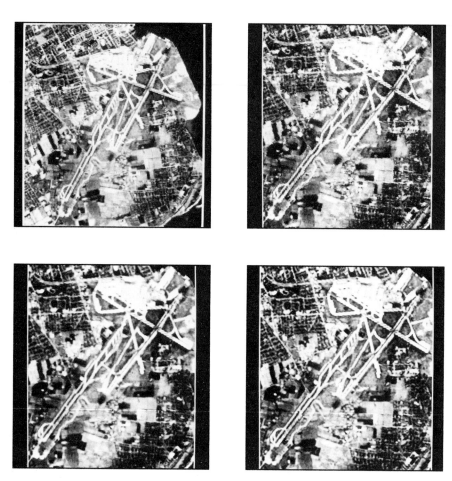

Figure 71. : Results of a geometric correction showing the effects of the different resampling methods. The input image, upper left, has been somewhat expanded and rotated counterclockwise. Nearest neighbor is in the upper right, bilinear interpolation in the lower left, and cubic convolution in the lower right.

Notice that they give the same output geometry. It is the impulse response of the resampling filter that they change.

6.5 Measuring the Accuracy of a Registration

Given that we can transform images to change their geometry and cause them to align with some reference, it is sometimes interesting to know how accurate the alignment is; that is, we would like to have a measure of how well the new geometry matches that of the reference. In case of a model that uses control points, one measure that is sometimes used is the mean of the RSS residuals of the fit that produced the model coefficients as listed in equation (6.1). Let us rewrite this equation as:

$$r(m) = d((k_m, l_m), M(i_m, j_m))$$

showing that the residual is the Euclidean distance in the input image from (k_m, l_m) to the mapped location $M(i_m, j_m)$. See Figure 72(a). However, these residuals are not a reliable measure. In many cases, they may be forced as small as desired simply by choosing higher order models. With ten control points, a bivariate third degree polynomial model, which has ten coefficients, will provide an exact fit with all zero residuals, regardless of the accuracy of the points and the resulting registration. The residuals should only be used as a measure if there are many more points in the fit than there are coefficients that are fit, and if it can be assumed that the model, polynomial or otherwise, is adequate to characterize the physical distortion to be removed.

Another possibility is to select additional "test points" in both the input and reference image. These are not used in the model fitting, but their residuals are computed and used to measure the model accuracy.

If an interpolation grid is used in the resampling, it may introduce additional errors. This is normally a very small error, and needs to be considered only if there is the possibility that the grid is not spaced finely enough compared to the derivatives of the model. To account for this error, the residuals of the control points used in the fit and/or the additional test points used for checking can be computed as:

$$r(m) = d((k_m, l_m), I(i_m, j_m))$$

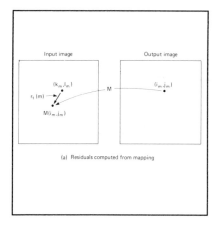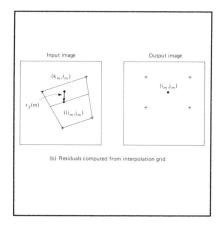

Figure 72. Methods of computing the residuals from a deformation model: (a) The residual for a control point computed directly from the model, and (b) the residual computed to include the component due to the interpolation grid.

where (k_m, l_m) is still the location of the m-th point in the input image, but here $I(i_m j_m)$ is the interpolated position of $(i_m j_m)$ in the input image. It is found using the interpolation grid and the equations for bilinear interpolation (Figure 67) and is shown in Figure 72(b).

These measures using control point and test point residuals are possible to compute before doing the resampling, and, as mentioned in the section describing the fitting, are often used in an iterative process to refine the set of control points, identify mislocated points, and so on, to arrive at a good fit.

Now let us assume the output image has been generated. Then there are additional ways to measure its accuracy. We will consider the case of an image-to-image registration. Let R be the reference image, I the input image, and C the corrected version of I which should geometrically match R.

A simple visual method to check the quality is to display the difference image $R - C$. Misregistrations will appear as black-white shadows as in Figure 73.

A quantitative method to check the accuracy is to measure in each of R and C the location of a new set of points well distributed over the images, and from these, derive some statistical measure on the average misregistration error. However, in case we are inter-

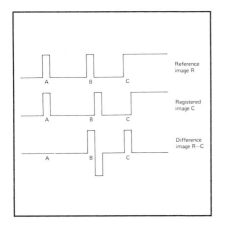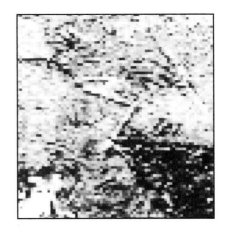

Figure 73. Misregistration shadows in a registered image: Part (a) illustrates why the shadows appear in a difference image, and (b) is an example. The horizontal V-shaped shadow shows that the corrected output image is below and to the right of the input image in this area.

ested in high, sub-pixel levels of accuracy, say 0.1 to 0.5 pixel, a problem arises in measuring an individual point. The measurement error for any given point may be about the same order as the error to be measured, so we need some way of separating the measurement error from the true, geometric error. Let o be the observed or measured error at a point. We will assume it is made up of the true geometric error g plus the measurement error m:

$$o = g + m$$

If we have measurements from many points, we may compute the variance of o:

$$\sigma^2(o) = \sigma^2(g + m) = \sigma^2(g) + \sigma^2(m) \tag{6.4}$$

where we have assumed the error components g and m are uncorrelated. It is $\sigma^2(g)$ that we would like to know as our measure of image geometric quality. If we further assume the true geometric errors are slowly varying over the image and thus constant within a given small region, we can estimate the measurement error by making many measurements in the region. Assuming the geometric errors are constant in such a region[4], the variance of this error component is zero in the region, and $\sigma^2(o) = \sigma^2(m)$. Then we can easily solve equation (6.4) for $\sigma^2(g)$. The procedure is as follows [28]:

1. Make a first set of measurements by selecting points in R and locating the same points in C in each of several small regions of the image, the boxes of Figure 74. Let r be the number of regions and n_i the number of measurements in the i-th region. Also let (k_{ij}, l_{ij}) be the coordinates of the j-th point in the i-th region in R, and (k'_{ij}, l'_{ij}) the coordinates in C. The measurements may be done manually or by correlation: a window from R at location (k,l) is correlated with a search area from C centered on $(k;l)$.

2. Considering the line coordinate first, compute the observed errors and variances in each region:

$$o_{ij} = k_{ij} - k'_{ij} \qquad \sigma^2(o_i) = \frac{\displaystyle\sum_{j=1}^{n_i}(o_{ij} - \bar{o}_{ij})^2}{n_i - 1}$$

where $\bar{o}_{ij}$ is the mean of o_{ij} in region i. The geometric error is assumed constant in the region, so $\sigma^2(m_i) = \sigma^2(o_i)$, and the above formula gives us an estimate of the measurement error in region i.

3. Combine the measurement error variances from each region as:

$$\hat{\sigma}^2(m) = \frac{\displaystyle\sum_{i=1}^{r}(n_i - 1)\,\sigma^2(m_i)}{\displaystyle\sum_{i=1}^{r}(n_i - 1)}$$

4

    The assumption that the geometric errors are constant in a small region is reasonable for errors due to perspective and view angle, the errors from a fish-eye lens, and so on, and is valid for most imaging systems including satellite mounted sensors. An example where it is not valid is for images from aircraft mounted sensors, which often have a large, rapidly varying error components due to sensor movement from atmospheric turbulence and aircraft motion. Here the geometric errors are not constant even over small regions.

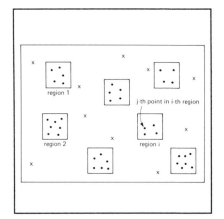 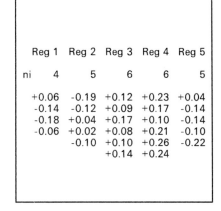

Figure 74. Measuring the accuracy of a registration: (a) The regions in which several measurements are made are shown as boxes, and the second set of measurements as x's. (b) Sample measurements for ANOVA computation.

to give a global estimate of the variance due to the measurement process.

4. Now locate a second set of points throughout the image, the xs of Figure 74, giving points (k_s, l_s) and (k'_s, l'_s), $s = 1, 2, \ldots, n_s$. Compute the observed line errors and error variance:

$$o_s = k_s - k'_s \qquad \sigma^2(o_s) = \frac{\sum_{s=1}^{n_s}(o_s - \bar{o}_s)^2}{n_s - 1}$$

5. Now estimate the true geometric error in the line coordinate as the observed error minus the estimated measurement error:

$$\sigma^2(g) = \sigma^2(o_s) - \hat{\sigma}^2(m)$$

This is the result we wanted. The calculations are repeated for the sample coordinates and, if desired, the two may be combined into one error measure as:

$$\sigma^2(g_{total}) = \sigma^2(g_{line}) + \sigma^2(g_{sample})$$

The method used two sets of measurements, and the idea was to subtract from the total variance of the second set the variance due to the measurement process computed in the first. The Analysis of Variance (ANOVA) technique [29] is a statistical method designed to do just this: separate the variance in a given set of measurements into its components. Using ANOVA, an estimate of the measurement error and the true geometric error can be obtained from a single set of measurements, one like the first set above with a number of measurements in each of several regions. The derivation of the results requires a fair amount of statistics, and we only state the results. For r regions, and n_i measurements in the i-th region, we assume $o_{ij} = g_i + m_{ij}$. That is, the error at point j in region i is made up of a fixed geometric error g_i for the region, plus a variable measurement error m_{ij}. Then ANOVA estimates $\sigma^2(g)$ as

$$\sigma^2(g) = \left(\frac{1}{k_0}\right)\left(\frac{S_2}{r-1} - \frac{S_1}{n-r}\right)$$

where

$$S_1 = \sum_{i=1}^{r}\sum_{j=1}^{n_i} o_{ij} - \sum_{i=1}^{r}\frac{p_i^2}{n_i} \qquad S_2 = \sum_{i=1}^{r}\left(\frac{p_i^2}{n_i}\right) - \frac{Q^2}{n}$$

$$p_i = \sum_{j=1}^{n_i} o_{ij} \qquad Q = \sum_{i=1}^{r} p_i \qquad k_0 = \frac{n^2 - \sum_{i=1}^{r} n_i^2}{n(r-1)} \qquad n = \sum n_i$$

An estimate for the measurement error is also given by the method and is equal to:

$$\sigma^2(m) = \frac{S_1}{n-r}$$

As an example using ANOVA, suppose that the measurements of line displacements between corresponding points in R and C shown in Figure 74 on page 155(b) have been made. From the table val-

156

ues, it is straightforward to compute $\sigma(g) = 0.11$ $(\sigma^2(g) = 0.01139)$ and $\sigma^2(m) = 0.08$ $(\sigma^2(m) = 0.006234)$, so that for this case the estimated geometric error has a standard deviation of about one tenth of a pixel, and the estimated measurement error is slightly less.

6.6 A Registration Method Based on Local Models

The registration method described earlier used a deformation model valid over the entire image. This is suitable for most medical and satellite images, and for many other cases. However, if the distortions in an image are irregular, it may be necessary to use higher order models, models with trigonometric terms (which are difficult to use in fitting routines), or more complete physical models of the imaging process. As an alternative, an accurate registration can be obtained in many cases by using low order polynomial models that are defined locally. The idea is illustrated in one dimension in Figure 75, where a function is approximated with local linear models. For use in registration, the image is divided into a set of regions and a model is computed in each region. However, as shown in the figure, one of the problems with local models is that discontinuities may be introduced at the boundaries.

One way of implementing a local modelling is to compute a local, polynomial model at each point of the interpolation grid described in section "Interpolation Grids" on page 140, and each grid point is mapped by its own polynomial. This avoids the boundary problem because it does not define regions of the image, but interpolates between every grid point. Each local polynomial is computed by a weighted least squares fit to the surrounding control points, weighting closer points more heavily. Let the grid be defined in the output image as the cross product $E \times F$ of a set E of line coordinates and a set F of sample coordinates:

$$E \times F = \{(e_i, f_j) : e_i \in E \text{ and } f_j \in F\}$$

Then for grid point (e_i, f_j), the line polynomial Q_{ij} is computed to minimize:

$$||W_{ij}(MQ_{ij} - K)||^2$$

where M, Q_{ij}, and K are defined as for the global polynomials, and the elements $w_{ij}(m,m)$ of the diagonal weighting matrix W are computed as:

$$w_{ij}(m,m) = \frac{1}{d((e_i, f_j),(k_m, l_m))^p}$$

where $d((a,b),(c,d))$ is the Euclidean distance between (a,b) and (c,d). $w_{ij}(m,m)$ weights the m-th control point based on the inverse of its distance to the grid point. p is a parameter controlling the weight of the control points: the larger p, the more relative weight is given to the closer points.

The least squares solution is given by

$$Q_{ij} = (M^T W_{ij}^2 M)^{-1} M^T W_{ij}^2 K$$

and a similar fit, replacing K by L gives R_{ij}. Two other parameters are:

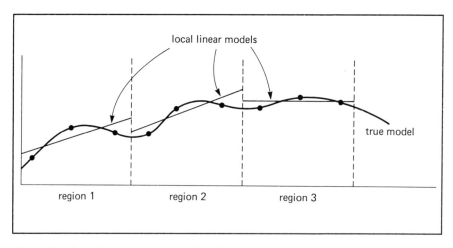

Figure 75.   Local linear models in one dimension.

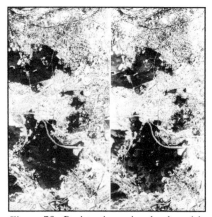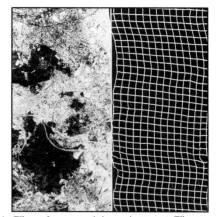

Figure 76. Registration using local models: (a) The reference and input images. The geometric differences are small but occur throughout the images. (b) The corrected image, and a regular grid transformed using the same correction. SPOT images courtesy of GDTA, Toulouse, France.

1. d_{min} is a threshold value such that if $d((e_{ij}, f_{ij}), (k_m, l_m)) < d_{min}$, then $w_{ij} = d_{min}$. This prevents points very close to a grid point from having an excessive (or infinite) weight.

2. n_c is used to limit the fitting to the closest n_c control points. Thus M varies with each grid point, becoming M_{ij}, and has n_c rows. K and L are n_c element vectors. Because in most cases, distance points contribute very little to the fit, using n_c significantly improves the speed of computation and may also improve the accuracy by omitting distance and irrelevant points.

Once they are computed, Q_{ij} and R_{ij} are evaluated at grid point (e_i, f_j) to obtain (h_{ij}, k_{ij}), the input image location of the grid point:

$$h_{ij} = Q_{ij}(e_i, f_j) \qquad k_{ij} = R_{ij}(e_i, f_j)$$

Because the fit is repeated at each grid point, this local fitting is computationally expensive. However, in a case where this was used, registering the two images of simulated SPOT data shown in Figure 76(a), the average displacement between points in the corrected image and in the reference image was reduced from 3.6 pixels for a global model to 0.4 pixels for a local model. Part (b) shows the corrected result (the correction is most noticeable along the edges), and a grid corrected identically. The irregularities shown by the grid cannot be modelled with a global polynomial.

6.7   Image-to-Image Registration

Many registrations are done to force two images to align with each other. This allows a pixel-by-pixel difference image to be made, changes detected, and so forth. To obtain the two registered images, two choices are available. The two images could be registered to a common reference, or one of the images could be registered directly to match the other. Higher accuracies can be obtained by using the second method. As an example, cartographers, geologists, and other users often require that two images be registered to a particular map projection such as Universal Transverse Mercator (UTM) as well as to each other. Let I1 and I2 be the two images, and assume that an image can be registered to UTM with an accuracy of σ_1. Then, using the first method, if I1 is registered to UTM with accuracy σ_1 giving I1′, and I2 is registered, giving I2′, the errors between them will add in an RSS sense, and the accuracy of I2′ relative to I1′ will be:

$$\sqrt{\sigma_1^2 + \sigma_1^2} = \sqrt{2}\,\sigma_1$$

Instead of registering each of I1 and I2 to the UTM reference, if I1 is registered to UTM to give I1′, and I2 is registered to match I1′, giving I2*, then I2* will match I1′ with an accuracy of σ_1, better by a factor of $\sqrt{2}$. See Figure 77. The error of I2* relative to UTM will be $\sqrt{2}\,\sigma_1$. However, the changes between the two images will be more apparent in the I2* version, and this is the critical point for the users.

In fact, the registration of I2 to I1′ is an image-to-image registration, not an image-to-map registration. As such, correlation may be used to find the control points and, in this case of images in similar wavelengths and pixel resolution, correlations are typically more accurate than manually found control points. Thus the error between I2* and I1′ is σ_2 where $\sigma_2 < \sigma_1$, whereas in the original method, the error was $\sqrt{2}\,\sigma_1$. For LANDSAT MSS data for which this operation

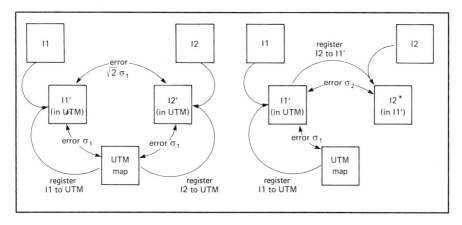

Figure 77. Two alternative ways of doing an image-to-image registration: Left: Both may be corrected to a common reference. Right: One may be corrected directly to match (a corrected version of) the other.

is typical, σ_2 is on the order of 0.2 pixels, σ_1 on the order of 0.4 pixels, and an improvement in relative accuracy of more than a factor of two can be achieved.

6.8 Problems in Geometric Transformations

From the previous sections, it is clear that the methods of digital image registration are well developed and that high geometric accuracies can be achieved. Factors that must be considered when doing a registration are:

1. The form of the mapping from output-to-input (or input-to-output). Because the monic polynomials 1, x, y, xy, x^2, y^2, ... are well understood and easy to use in mathematical analysis and computer programs, they are often used for the deformation model. However, they can exactly model only certain types of deformations, as listed below:

$$\text{Translation} \qquad L(i,\ j) = l_0 + i$$
$$K(i,\ j) = k_0 + j$$

Above plus scale change	$L(i, j) = l_0 + l_1 i$ $K(i, j) = k_0 + k_1 j$
Above plus Rotation	$L(i, j) = l_0 + l_1 i + l_2 j$ $K(i, j) = k_0 + k_1 j + k_2 i$
Above plus Shear	$L(i, j) = l_0 + l_1 i + l_2 j + l_3 ij$ $K(i, j) = k_0 + k_1 j + k_2 i + k_3 ij$

Other deformations may require other forms of a model. The geometry of an aircraft mounted sensor flying at altitude h is given in Figure 78(a). Input sample number l is proportional to the angle θ and output sample number j to flat ground distance d, and the model:

$$\tan(\theta) = \frac{d}{h} \quad \text{or} \quad \tan(c_1 l) = \frac{c_2 j}{h} \quad \text{giving} \quad j = \frac{h \tan(c_1 l)}{c_2}$$

is appropriate. Depending on the range of θ, modelling l as a polynomial in j is a poor choice since it could require many terms and, if control points are used, could be unstable for small errors in their locations. Thus a physical model is frequently a better choice than a polynomial. The disadvantage of the physical model is that it must be derived. A polynomial model is simple and general. Once derived, it may be applied to many cases, and will often provide a good approximation. If the polynomial model is to be used, the choice of terms must be balanced between sufficient terms to model the deformations present, and not too many terms, which permits unrealistic oscillations.

2. Adequate control points. Assuming that control points are to be used to derive the mapping, and that the form of the mapping, either polynomial or model, adequately describes the deformation, the accuracy of the mapping and the correction will depend on the accuracy, number, and distribution of the control points. Normally, control points selected around the edges of the image are the best, as suggested by the linear example in

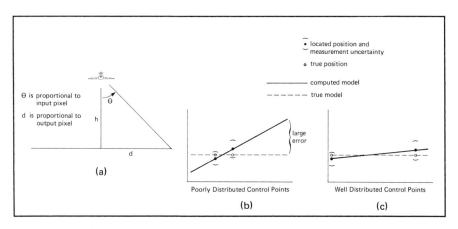

Figure 78. : (a) Example geometry for deriving an output-to-input mapping for an aircraft mounted sensor. (b) and (c) illustrate why control points near the edges of an image are usually best.

Figure 78(b) and (c). The same is true in the two dimensions of deformation models and is actually worse for high order models. In such a case, regions in an image with no control points can droop or oscillate in the corrected image.

3. Finding control points manually can be a tedious task. Finding them automatically, even in scenes of the same resolution and wavelength, can be difficult due to such factors as illumination changes. In agricultural images, fields may change dramatically as new crops are planted, ripen, and are harvested. Edges may be more stable than pixel value, so in some cases, an edge detector is applied to the search and window arrays and the correlation is done on these edge images. Residuals from the control point fit provide a first level check on the control point accuracy, and should always be checked. Control points with high residuals may need to be relocated or omitted. However, an isolated control point with a high residual is often better kept than deleted for the reasons described above in (2).

4. Registering images of significantly different resolutions typically requires manually located control points. Also, an alternate re-sampling method may be best. If the pixels of a low resolution

image correspond, for example, to 5 x 5 blocks of high resolution pixels, cubic convolution, which interpolates to sub-pixel values, is not a good choice to resample the high resolution image down to match it to the low resolution image. Rather some form of 5 x 5 averaging is better, giving output pixels corresponding to the same ground area.

5. Some components of the geometric deformation are local and must be handled differently than the components modelled by the deformation models described so far. One local component is the effect of topography in remote sensing data. The different heights of mountains and valleys induce displacements in the input image data when not viewed directly from above. If a digital elevation model is available, it may be used to compute a final pixel-by-pixel displacement to the input sample location at which to resample to compensate for the displacement.

6.9   Discussion

Unlike the filtering and segmentation operations described in previous chapters, results from geometric transformations and registrations may be quantitatively measured and absolute accuracies assigned. The methods of registration are well-developed and in most cases high accuracies, up to 0.1 pixels for satellite images, may be obtained if the deformation is adequately modelled and/or sufficient control points are located. Such high accuracies are not usually attainable or necessary for medical images because of the inherent blur in the images.

The task of registering two images, even with similar wavelengths and pixel resolutions, may still be formidable since many control points may be needed, or a complex model necessary to describe the geometry of the deformation. Nevertheless, with time and patience these may be done. For images of different wavelengths and/or resolutions, in which objects appear differently or different sets of objects appear, manually assisted methods are usually necessary and results are not as accurate.

6.10 Questions and Problems

1. Derive the equations for the cubic convolution interpolating function. It is sketched in the lower left of Figure 69, and consists of the two cubics:

$$f(x) = a_0 + a_1 x + a_2 x^2 + a_3 x^3 \qquad 0 \le x < 1$$

and
$$g(x) = b_0 + b_1 x + b_2 x^2 + b_3 x^3 \qquad 1 \le x \le 2$$

The eight unknowns are the a_i and the b_i. Using the following conditions, derive these eight unknowns:

$$f(0) = 1 \quad f(1) = 0 \quad g(1) = 0 \quad g(2) = 0 \quad f'(0) = 0 \quad g'(2) = 0$$

$$f'(1) = g'(1) \quad f''(0) < 0 \quad f''(1) > 0 \quad \int_0^1 f(x) \; + \; \int_1^2 g(x) \; = \frac{1}{2}$$

You will find that these conditions do not lead to a unique solution. One way of expressing the results is that the solution is unique if b_3 which must be in the range (-3,0), is specified. The standard form of cubic convolution uses $b_3 = -1$.

2. An image is digitally resampled to shift it to the left by one quarter of a pixel. (If polynomials are used, $Q(i, j) = i$ and $R(i, j) = j + 0.25$.) Later it is resampled to shift it back. Suppose that this resampling for shifting is repeated many times. What will happen to the image if nearest neighbor resampling is used? Bilinear interpolation? Cubic convolution?

3. The function $f(x) = a \sin \pi x$ is sampled at points $(\pi/10)t$ for $t = 0,1,2, \dots$. From the samples, the function is reconstructed. What is the maximum error in the reconstructed signal if nearest neighbor is used? Bilinear interpolation?

4. By inspection, define an input and output grid that will magnify a 256 x 256 image to size 512 x 512. What is the minimum number of grid points needed to avoid errors in the bilinear interpolation mapping output points to the input?

7.0   Classification

In this chapter we consider statistical image classification. In general terms, the objective is, given a set of objects, assign each object to one of a set of classes. For our purposes, the objects are the pixels in an image, and the classes are the various categories occurring in the image. The most common application is to remote sensing images in which the categories are classes such as wheat, barley, and other crop types, water, urban areas, and so on. Classification may also be thought of as a labelling problem: labelling each object with a class label.

In the first sections, we will not often be concerned with a pixel's spatial coordinates. However it will be important to distinguish between a pixel p and its values v. We normally consider multiband data, so the values of a pixel can be represented as a vector:

$$v = \begin{bmatrix} v_1 \\ v_2 \\ \cdot \\ \cdot \\ \cdot \\ v_n \end{bmatrix}$$

v_i is the value of p in the i-th band. These components are often referred to as features because in statistical decision theory, from which the mathematics is taken, they often represent physical features of an object, such as weight or area. For image classification, the features include the original band values, as well as generated bands such as band ratios or the principal component bands (see appendix "Principal Components" on page 192). In this sense, feature becomes a more general term than band. Another point of notation is that we use $c(i)$ to denote the classes to which a pixel can be assigned.

There are two basic categories of classification methods: supervised and unsupervised. In the supervised methods, the user "supervises" the process by initially selecting some pixels from each possible class. From these, the classification algorithm determines what each class "looks like", and then assigns each pixel of the image to one of the classes. In the unsupervised methods, the classes are determined within the algorithm by locating clusters in pixel space[5], and assuming each cluster corresponds to a class. The problem becomes one of cluster identification. A final step in the unsupervised case, which must be done by the user, is to decide which clusters represent which physical classes such as wheat, water, etc. We consider first the supervised methods.

7.1   Supervised Classification

Bayesian Maximum Likelihood Classification

Bayesian Maximum Likelihood Classification is a well-developed method from statistical decision theory that has been applied to problems of classifying image data. To describe the method, we begin with an example. Suppose we have a one band image of a coastal area containing land and water, and we want to classify each pixel as either land, class 1, or water, class 2. The result will be a "class map" or image in which each pixel has a code, 1 or 2, corresponding respectively to land and water.

To assign each pixel to one of the classes, we need a "decision rule". For example, a trivial decision rule is:

---

[5]

Pixel space is the space in which a pixel with value v_1 in band 1, v_2 in band 2, ... is represented by the point $(v_1, v_2, ...)$.

Assign all pixels on the left half of the image to class water. Assign all on the right to land

But this is an arbitrary rule with no apparent justification. A more reasonable rule can be derived if we look at the pixel values in several areas known to be land, and in several other areas known to be water. Then we may arrive at a decision rule such as:

Assign all pixels whose value is less than 18 to water. Assign all others to land.

Here the decision rule is just a threshold, identical to the thresholds described in "Thresholding" on page 113. The problem will become more interesting as the number of classes and number of bands increases, but it is still one of determining good decision rules. The Bayesian Maximum Likelihood method is one way to derive the decision rules. The explanation that follows is in three parts. The first continues the above example to introduce more of the concepts. The second gives a brief but more precise statistical statement of the method, and the third is a list of steps that are followed to apply it.

Returning to the example, suppose that we look again at several areas known to be water and several known to be land. These are called training areas, because they will be used to "train" the classifier. Let us compute the histograms $h_l(v)$ of the land pixels, and $h_w(v)$ of the water pixels, giving the plots shown in Figure 79(a). Now we could classify each pixel p in the image by using the rule: For v the value of p, assign p to water if $h_w(v)$ is greater than $h_l(v)$. Assign p to land otherwise. (Notice that land wins in case of a tie, but this is unimportant.) Referring to Figure 79, a pixel with value a is assigned to water, and b and c are assigned to land.

But there is an obvious problem. If there are more pixels in the training area for land, its histogram is generally larger so it is more heavily weighted. This is fixed by normalizing the histograms to have unit area, giving $H_l(v)$ and $H_w(v)$, Figure 79(b). In this case, a and c are still classified as water and land as before, but b has moved from land to water.

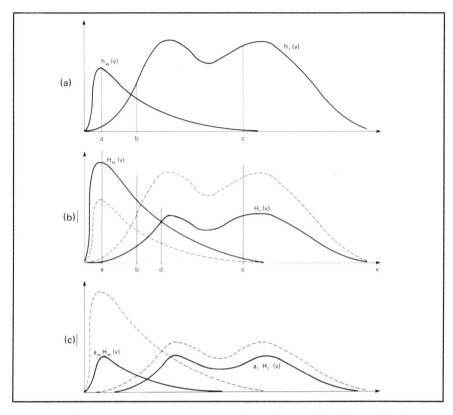

Figure 79. Sample class histograms for a two class problem: (a) The original histograms over the training areas. (b) The normalized histograms. (c) The normalized histograms scaled by the a priori probabilities.

Now suppose that, by looking at existing maps or just by looking at the image, it is clear that most of the image is land, say 70%, and only 30% is water. This means that if we pick a pixel at random, its probability of being land is 0.7. These percentages give the probability of a pixel belonging to a class even before looking at its value, and are called the a priori probabilities. For pixel with value d in Figure 79(b), this might lead us to pick class land. In fact, it suggests that we should weight the entire histograms as shown in Figure 79(c) with these a priori probabilities a_l and a_w.

By including the a priori probabilities to weight the curves, we have the decision rule:

For v the value of p, assign p to water if $a_w H_w(v)$ is greater than $a_l H_l(v)$. Assign p to land otherwise.

This is the basic maximum likelihood decision rule. Its extension to multiple classes, using one histogram per class, and to multiple bands, using n-dimensional histograms, is conceptually straightforward.

We are now ready for our second step: to state the results somewhat more precisely. We start with some notation and two results from statistical decision theory. The notation is:

$q(i)$: The a priori probability that any pixel belongs to class i. This is the probability, assumed known before the classification starts, that a pixel, chosen at random, belongs to class i. In the example above, these are a_l and a_w, the 70% and 30% probabilities.

$q(v|i)$: This is read "the probability of v given i." It is the class conditional probability density function for class i, or the probability that a pixel from class i has value v.

$q(i|v)$: This is read "the probability of i given v." It is the probability that a pixel with value v is in class i.

$q(v)$: The sum of the $q(v|i)$ over all i. This is simply a normalization factor and is not a probability.

The first result we need is Bayes Formula:

$$q(i|v) = \frac{q(v|i)q(i)}{q(v)}$$

for the terms as defined above. This formula gives a means of computing the probability of i given v from the opposite probability, that of v given i. The second result is the decision rule we will use. It is called Bayes Decision rule, and stated in terms of pixels, it is:

Given a pixel with value v and, for each class i, the probability $q(i|v)$ that the pixel is from class i, then the best class to assign the pixel to is the class for which $q(i|v)$ is maximum.

A little thought shows this to be a rather intuitive and natural rule. In addition, it is shown by Bayesian theory to be the "Bayes optimal" rule under appropriate assumptions. Bayes optimal means that the overall probability of error of classification is minimized. As for the appropriate assumptions, the key one has to do with the consequences of making a bad classification---things like: Is it worse to incorrectly classify a pixel from class i or to incorrectly classify a pixel from class j? Do some misclassifications have extra bad consequences? The assumption that leads to the maximum likelihood rule is that all bad classifications are equally bad, and none worse than others. Under other assumptions, such as those favoring certain classes, other Bayes classifiers may be derived.

Putting the results together, to use the Bayes maximum likelihood rule, we assign pixel p to class i for which $q(i|v)$ is maximum. This requires $q(i|v)$ for all i. We do not originally have these, but, by Bayes theorem, they can be computed from $q(v|i)$ and $q(i)$. We do not have these either, but they can be estimated. We estimate $q(v|i)$ as the normalized histogram of class i, and we estimate $q(i)$ from physical considerations of the problem we are solving such as estimates from available maps, previous year's results for agricultural studies, or simply estimates from viewing the image. Also, because the denominator $q(v)$ in Bayes Rule is the same for all i, it may be ignored in selecting the maximum $q(i|v)$. In this case, the Bayes Rule is exactly the decision rule we arrived at in our two-class water and land example, so both the example and the theory have led to the same method.

The third step is now to state the method as a sequence of conceptual steps necessary to classify an image. These steps are:

1. Select training areas for each candidate class. These are areas known (or assumed) to contain pixels in the class. In general, the more training data per class the better, since this should give a truer representation of the class histogram.

2. Compute the n dimensional histogram for the training data for each class, where n is the number of features, and normalize the histograms, giving $H_i(v)$. Use these as estimates of the conditional probability density functions $q(v|i)$ giving the probability that a pixel has value v given it belongs to class i. There is one $q(v|i)$ for each of the i classes.

3. Estimate the a priori probabilities $q(i)$ and use them to scale the $q(v|i)$, giving $q(v|i)q(i)$. (By the previous step, this is $q(i)H_i(v)$.) This is the probability that a pixel has value v given it is in class i times the probability the pixel is in class i.

4. Classify each pixel in the image by computing, for each class i, $q(i|v)$ as:

$$q(i|v) = \frac{q(v|i)q(i)}{q(v)}$$

In practice, we drop the denominator, which is the same for all i, and compute the unnormalized product $g(i|v)$:

$$g(i|v) = q(v|i)q(i)$$

To classify the pixel, assign it to the class i for which $g(i|v)$ is maximum.

Steps 1, 2, and 3 are only done once, then step 4 is applied to each pixel in the image to produce the output or classified image.

The term $g(i|v)$ is normally considered as a function of v, and is a probability (although unnormalized). However, when considered as a function of i, it is called the likelihood function, and this gives the method its name: maximum likelihood classification.

The steps above outline the basic approach. However, there is a problem implementing them in a computer program. In step 2, $q(v|i)$ was computed as the normalized n dimensional histogram over the training data. If there are m possible pixel values per band and n bands, each $q(v|i)$ requires a table of size m^n and a k class problem requires tables of size km^n. In an 8 class, 4 band problem with pixel values from 0 to 127 in each band, more than two billion words of computer memory are needed: 8×128^4. Although some form of memory partitioning or storage management could be implemented in software, these can be cumbersome. The problem is avoided by representing the $q(v|i)$ not as n dimensional histograms but as functions for which only a few parameters need to be stored. The method is then called a parametric classifier. Of course, the parameters must be calculated or estimated. The most common choice of functional representation of $q(v|i)$ is as Gaussian distributions in which, for the one dimensional case, the parameters that must be estimated are the mean and standard deviation of the distribution. The general form of a one dimensional Gaussian with mean m, standard deviation σ, and normalized to have area one is:

$$\frac{1}{\sqrt{2\pi}\,\sigma}e^{-\frac{1}{2}\frac{(x-m)^2}{\sigma^2}}$$

In our case, this becomes:

$$q(v|i) = \frac{1}{\sqrt{2\pi}\,\sigma_i}e^{-\frac{(x-m_i)^2}{2\sigma_i^2}} \tag{7.1}$$

where m_i and σ_i are the mean and standard deviation of the i-th class. For an n band problem, m_i becomes an n dimensional vector of means, σ_i becomes an $n \times n$ covariance matrix Σ_i, and the scaling factor becomes $(2\pi)^{n/2}$. In this form, the memory requirements are greatly reduced.

Values for the class mean and covariance matrices must be obtained. There is no way to compute them exactly, and they can only be estimated. Decision theory provides at least two different ways to estimate the parameters, one of which is called maximum likelihood parameter estimation[6]. In this method, the mean and standard deviation are taken as the mean and standard deviation for

---

6

This second use of the term maximum likelihood may be confusing. What this is saying is that the maximum likelihood method may be used to estimate the parameters for a maximum likelihood classification.

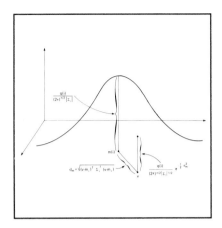

Figure 80. Evaluating the likelihood of a pixel belonging to a class: The surface is the normalized and scaled class conditional probability density function, modelled as a Gaussian.

the corresponding training data, and this is the method most often used in image processing applications.

To perform the classification of an image using this parametric form, we use the training data to compute the n dimensional vector mean and the $n \times n$ covariance matrix Σ_i for each class. Then for each pixel, we evaluate:

$$g(v \mid i) = q(i) \frac{1}{(2\pi)^{\frac{n}{2}} |\Sigma_i|^{\frac{1}{2}}} e^{-\frac{1}{2}(v - m_i)^T \Sigma_i^{-1}(v - m_i)} \tag{7.2}$$

for each class i, and assign p to the class for which $g(i \mid v)$ is maximum. For a given i this is illustrated in Figure 80. The term

$$(v - m_i)^T \Sigma_i^{-1}(v - m_i)$$

in the exponent is a weighted distance from v to m_i (weighted by Σ_i^{-1}) called the Mahalanobis distance; the term

$$\frac{1}{(2\pi)^{\frac{n}{2}} |\Sigma_i|^{\frac{1}{2}}}$$

is the normalization factor to give the Gaussian distribution a unit area/volume; and $q(i)$ is the a priori probability to scale the result. Although equation 7.2 is the basic form of our parametric classifier,

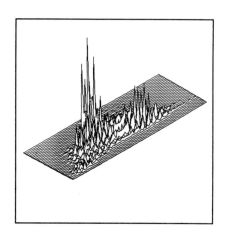

Figure 81. Example distribution computed from training data: In this case, the distribution is poorly modelled as a Gaussian.

for computational efficiency, we can simplify it. We avoid the exponential by taking the logarithm, and we drop the constant term. The result is the simpler expression:

$$g(i\,|\,v) = \log_e q(i) - \frac{1}{2}\log_e|\Sigma_i| - \frac{1}{2}(v - m_i)^T\Sigma_i^{-1}(v - m_i) \quad (7.3)$$

This is the form normally used in computer implementations, and in this case, p is assigned to the class for which $g(i\,|\,v)$ is minimum. With this, we have a complete method for doing a parametric Bayesian classification.

We now look at three aspects of using such a classifier.

Gaussian Assumption. The assumption of the Gaussian form to approximate the class distributions may or may not be valid. Figure 81 shows a two dimensional plot of the distribution of training data for a class taken from an actual project. The distribution is poorly modelled as a Gaussian. The most common solution in such a case is to split the class into subclasses, which may be more nearly Gaussian, perform the classification, and then recombine the subclasses. Using other non-Gaussian forms of distributions is difficult both analytically and in implementation. In any case, the distribution of the training data should at least be checked visually before using them in a classification.

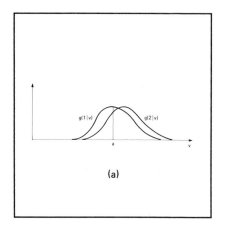 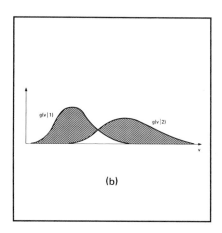

(a) (b)

Figure 82. : (a) Distributions for two classes with high overlap. A pixel with value a has a high likelihood of belonging to class 1 but may still easily belong to class 2. (b) Distributions for two classes showing the region (shaded) related to the J-M distance.

Thresholding the Output. In a maximum likelihood classification, each pixel is assigned to a class, and this is the class in which it has the greatest likelihood of belonging. A pixel that belongs to none of the classes and has a low likelihood of belonging to each of them, will still be assigned to whichever one has the maximum. What is needed is an "unclassified" category for pixels whose likelihood of belonging to any class is quite low. This can be done by saving and later thresholding the likelihoods. That is, as each pixel is classified, its computed class and likelihood of belonging to the class are both saved. Following the classification, a threshold can be specified (which is best if class dependent) and all pixels in a class whose likelihood of belonging to the class are less than the threshold are moved to the "unclassified" class.

Numerical Separation of the Classes. A good classification can be obtained only if the classes are numerically separated. If there is extensive overlap in their distributions, even a high likelihood value for a pixel does not give us confidence in its correct classification. Referring to Figure 82(a), pixel a has a high likelihood of belonging to class 1 but it is clear from the curves that it is still highly likely to belong to class 2. What is needed is some measure of class separability in order to assess the accuracy we can expect from a classifica-

177

tion. One such measure is the Jeffries-Matusita (J-M) distance. It provides a measure of the distance between two classes in a given set of bands. The distance between class i and class j is defined as:

$$\mathcal{J}_{ij} = \left(\int_v (\sqrt{q(v\,|\,i)} - \sqrt{q(v\,|\,j)})^2 \, dv \right)^{\frac{1}{2}}$$

The distributions of two classes are plotted in one dimension (corresponding to one band) in Figure 82(b), and the J-M distance is related, by the squares and square roots in the above equation, to the shaded area between the curves. The larger this area, the more separated the classes. The a priori probabilities are not included in the J-M distance and because $\int q(v\,|\,i) = 1$, the above integral is bounded by $\sqrt{2}$.

If multivariate normal distributions are assumed, the J-M distance can be computed as:

$$\mathcal{J}_{ij} = \sqrt{[2(1 - e^{-a})]}$$

where

$$a = \frac{1}{8}(m_i - m_j)^T \left(\frac{\Sigma_i + \Sigma_j}{2} \right)^{-1} (m_i - m_j) + \frac{1}{2} \log_e \left(\frac{|(\Sigma_i + \Sigma_j)/2|}{\sqrt{(|\Sigma_i|\,|\Sigma_j|)}} \right)$$

This daunting looking formula can be evaluated for each i and j, where i and j range over all classes, and by inspecting a table of $\mathcal{J}_{ij}$ we can have an idea of how well the classes are separated.

Each $\mathcal{J}_{ij}$ only gives a measure between two classes, although for any number of bands, and if we need a single measure of overall class separability for a given set of bands, an average pairwise J-M distance can be computed as:

$$\mathcal{J}_{ave} = \sum_i \sum_j q(i)q(j)\mathcal{J}_{ij}$$

This is the average J-M distance weighted by the a priori probabilities so that frequent classes are favored.

	A	B	C	D	E
A	0.0				
B	0.30	0.0			
C	0.56	0.46	0.0		
D	0.93	0.82	0.49	0.0	
E	0.80	0.73	0.39	0.28	0.0
F	0.78	0.74	0.41	0.35	0.13

J-M distance 2 bands

	A	B	C	D	E
A	0.0				
B	1.39	0.0			
C	1.36	0.50	0.0		
D	1.41	0.85	0.61	0.0	
E	1.41	0.82	0.64	0.32	0.0
F	1.39	0.34	0.43	0.46	0.46

J-M distance 3 bands

	A	B	C	D	E
A	0.0				
B	1.41	0.0			
C	1.41	0.65	0.0		
D	1.41	0.93	0.73	0.0	
E	1.41	0.90	0.78	0.38	0.0
F	1.41	0.85	0.68	0.53	0.51

J-M distance 4 bands

	A	B	C	D	E
A	0				
B	19	0			
C	19	2	0		
D	22	8	6	0	
E	23	10	9	2	0
F	21	6	4	4	5

Euclidean distance 4 bands

Figure 83. J-M distance computed over two, three, and four bands

The J-M distance can be used in two related ways. First, it gives an idea of which classes will be accurately classified. We can expect low accuracies for classes close to other classes, and high accuracies for isolated classes. Secondly, it helps in selecting additional bands. Because Bayesian classification can be applied to any number of bands, one standard technique to separate poorly separated classes is to include additional bands. The additional bands may be ratios of existing bands, or, especially for satellite data, they may be bands from another image of the same area taken at another date. (To be used, the data from the different dates must be precisely registered.) In fact, it is easy to generate many additional bands (see, for example, [35]), and the J-M distance can be computed using them to determine if they will help separate the classes.[7]

----

[7]

An exception is the principal components or other linear combinations. These can be used in place of, but generally not in addition to, the original bands. They add no new information---only, let us say, a new way of looking at the old information. Because they are not independent of the original bands, if they are included together with them in a classification, they may introduce singularities (for example, non-invertible matrices) in the computations.

Figure 83 shows an example of the J-M distance computed over 2, 3, and 4 bands using a fixed set of training data, and also gives the Euclidean distance between the class mean centers in the four band case. From the values in the table, we can see that only class A can be accurately classified using these bands. All other classes have considerable overlap. We can also see that classes A and D, which are not separated using only two bands, are fully separated by 3 bands. For these two classes, the fourth band is unnecessary. Finally, notice the inversion that can occur between Euclidean distance and J-M distance. The Euclidean distance between B and C is less than between E and F but the opposite is true for J-M distance.

The J-M distance is only one of many methods that may be used to measure class separability. The general problem, referred to as feature selection, is a large area of study in statistical decision theory.

Minimum Distance Classification

The Bayesian maximum likelihood classifier of the previous section is probably the most common method used to classify multiband image data. It is fairly expensive to run, and the parametric form using the Gaussian assumption for class distributions is sometimes troublesome. Other classification methods are possible, and to define an alternate classifier, the main requirement is to define the decision rules. One class of decision rules are "minimum distance" rules.

Let m_i be the mean value of the pixels in training class i. In an n feature problem, m_i is a point (or vector) in n dimensional space. Minimum distance classifiers assign a pixel to the class i for which the distance from the pixel value v to m_i is minimum. Different distance measures may be used, different measures having various theoretical or computational advantages. Two common ones are:

1. Euclidean distance:

$$d(v, m_i) = \sqrt{(v_1 - m_{i1})^2 + \cdots + (v_n - m_{in})^2}$$

180

It can be shown that this is a special case of the Bayesian classifier for multivariate Gaussian distributions in which the features are statistically independent, with equal variances, and the a priori probabilities are equal. The surfaces of equal likelihood are (hyper)spheres in feature space, centered at the class means.

2. "City block" or L1 distance:

$$d(v, m_i) = |v_1 - m_{i1}| + \cdots + |v_n - m_{in}|$$

Both of these are computationally faster than Bayesian classification but may sacrifice classification accuracy. A comparison of a Bayesian maximum likelihood and a minimum distance classification using L1 distance based on the same training data is shown in Figure 84. In this case, the distributions of the different classes were quite different: some had high variances and other had low. Because the variances are used in the parametric Bayesian classifier (see the comments following equation (7.2)), but not the minimum distance, the results are clearly different, and the Bayesian method is more accurate.

7.2 Unsupervised Classification

Methods of unsupervised classification attempt to find clusters in the distribution of the pixels in pixel space. Although clusters are often fairly easy for a human to identify in one and two dimensional plots, their centers and boundaries are difficult to identify mathematically, and cluster analysis is a field of study all its own.

One iterative clustering method is called the K-means algorithm. Expressed in terms for image data, it has the following steps. Initially the user supplies a set of means, or cluster centers, $m_1, m_2, m_3, \ldots$ (and thus implicitly the number of classes). Each m_i is a vector in n dimensional pixel space. Then

1. For each pixel in the image, assign the pixel to the class to whose mean it is closest.

2. Recompute the mean of each class as the average of the pixels assigned to it.

Figure 84. Comparison of Bayesian (left) and minimum distance classifications: The minimum distance classifier used the "city block" distance, and both used the same training data.

3. If any of the class means has changed significantly, go to step 1. Otherwise stop.

ISODATA, [32] and [33], is the name of a K-means type of algorithm that includes parameters to allow classes to be split and merged. The additional parameters are:

1. A threshold on the minimum distance between two cluster centers, so that two cluster centers close together are merged.
2. A threshold on the standard deviation within each band for each class, so that a cluster with too much variability is split in two. One way of doing the splitting is to define two new cluster centers at some given distance (another parameter) on either side of the old mean in the band of maximum standard deviation.
3. A minimum number of pixels in a cluster. Clusters with less than this minimum are dropped and their pixels assigned to other clusters. This avoids many small clusters.
4. A maximum number of clusters which can be merged at any iteration. This is needed to avoid over-merging.

Figure 85. Comparison of results from a Bayesian (left) and ISODATA (right) classification.

Even with these parameters, best results are usually obtained when running this unsupervised classifier in a "supervised" mode. In this case, after each iteration, the user views the results, adjusts parameters to control the splitting and merging, and stops the iterations when satisfactory classes have been obtained. An example of the results of an ISODATA clustering, together with the same data classified by a Bayesian classifier, are shown in Figure 85.

The advantage of an unsupervised classification such as ISODATA is that it tends to identify clusters in the pixel space that are numerically separable, whereas the advantage of supervised classification is that the classes that are used are meaningful to the user or analyst. (Compare the classes selected by a user and by ISODATA in Figure 85.) The methods may be combined by using the unsupervised clustering to check the numerical separability of the user defined classes prior to the supervised run. As an example, suppose that the training data for a certain class includes data from two different populations, such as samples of a crop type from the sunny and shady slope of a hill, and suppose further that the distribution may be accurately modelled as two Gaussians, but poorly modelled as one. Such a bimodal distribution can be checked visually in one and two bands using plots of one and two dimensional histograms,

183

but is difficult to detect in higher dimensions. If the data is considered as one class for a Bayesian parametric classifier using Gaussian distributions, the variance of the class will be inappropriately large and the classifier performance degraded. However, if the training data for each class is clustered with ISODATA, then the two subpopulations might be identified. These can then be split and used as separate classes for the supervised classifier, and recombined into a single crop type afterwards.

7.3 Using Spatial Information in Classification

One of the main deficiencies of all the classification methods described so far is that each pixel is treated independently with no consideration of its neighbors. Clearly, in most cases, there is a strong spatial dependency. One would not expect a random distribution of wheat, corn, soybean, and water pixels over an image, but rather groups of like pixels occurring together, corresponding to agricultural fields and bodies of water. Numerous methods are available to try to use this spatial dependency and in most cases they improve the results. One class of methods uses a segmentation technique to group sets of pixels together into larger units, and then makes a single classification on each unit. For example, the edge based method of "Segmentation" on page 113 could be applied to one band of the image to generate segments. Others methods classify each pixel and then as a postprocessing step, change individual pixels based on their class assignments and likelihoods and those of their neighbors. Two examples of this second type of postprocessing are:

Relaxation. The likelihoods of each pixel belonging to each class computed by a maximum likelihood classifier are used as the initial probabilities for a relaxation ("Relaxation" on page 121). By relaxing these probabilities, where compatibilities are positive for equal classes, and zero or negative for different classes, the classification of each pixel is made dependent on its neighbor's class assignments. An example was shown in Figure 61 on page 124.

However several problems arise in using relaxation. First, how should the input probabilities be normalized? As given by the maximum likelihood classifier, they are actually likelihoods and so do not sum to one as relaxation probabilities do. A simple pixel-by-pixel normalization can give distorted probabilities. As an example, suppose that in a two class problem, a pixel has likelihood 0.01 of belonging to class 1, and 0.09 of belonging to class 2. Simple normalization converts these to 0.1 and 0.9, and this pixel may then strongly influence its neighbors towards class 2 even though its initial likelihood was only 0.09 of belonging to the class. A second problem is in terminating the iterations of the relaxation. Most improvements are in the first iterations, say the first 10 [34], and the accuracy begins to decrease as some stage, so it is necessary to stop the iterations somehow. A final problem is the computational cost: relaxation is rather expensive.

Local adjustment of a priori probabilities. Another method of using spatial information in a classifier follows the intuitive idea that a pixel surrounded, for example, by wheat has a high probability of being wheat. The method uses a Bayesian maximum likelihood classifier, but varies the a priori probabilities locally based on neighborhood information. An initial classification using equal a priori probabilities is run, and the likelihoods of each pixel belonging to each class are saved. A second classification is run in which the a priori probabilities $q(i)$ become $q(i,k,l)$, functions of pixel coordinates k and l. Each $q(i,k,l)$ is computed as the average of the first-run likelihoods for class i in some neighborhood of (k,l). That is, the likelihood of the pixel at (k,l) belonging to class i in the second classification is computed as:

$$q(i \mid v) = q(v \mid i) q(i,k,l)$$

where the locally varying a priori value is computed as:

$$q(i,k,l) = \frac{\displaystyle\sum_{n(k,l)} L(i,k,l)}{\displaystyle\sum_{i}\sum_{n(k,l)} L(i,k,l)}$$

Figure 86. Using neighborhood information in a classification.: The original output of a Bayesian classification is on the left. The right image is the result when the a priori probabilities are locally adjusted based on neighborhood averages computed from the likelihoods of the left run.

$L(i,k,l)$ is the computed likelihood (the result of the first classification) for the pixel at (k,l) belonging to class i. $n(k,l)$ is some neighborhood of (k,l). By saving the $q(i|v)$, the method may be iterated. Figure 86 shows an example of one iteration, computing $q(i,k,l)$ over 3 x 3 neighborhoods, compared with an equal a priori maximum likelihood run.

7.4 Steps in a Complete Classification Task

We have now dealt with many of the algorithmic aspects of classification. However, performing a supervised classification is not a fixed, more-or-less automatic procedure, but an operation involving much interaction between the user and the computer system, and requiring many human decisions. In this section, we outline the steps in a representative classification job.

Let us assume the classification is to be done using multiband satellite data from two different dates. The first step is to acquire the data, and the seemingly simple step of getting good quality, cloud free images may be difficult. Once the data is in hand, we may perform one or more pre-processing and clean-up operations such as atmospheric correction, solar zenith angle normalization, and computation of principal components, ratios, or other generated bands. The data from the different dates must be precisely registered, and a good way to do this is to register one image to the final output geometry desired, and then register the remaining image to this one. Much of this can be done semi-automatically and with a high geometric accuracy.

Ground information must be obtained. The best source is data gathered by field work at the approximate time the image data was taken. Existing maps may be used for some classes, and others, say bodies of water, may be identified simply by looking at the image. Training fields in the image are selected by outlining them with a cursor in displays of the data, and assigned a name and class. Once they have been selected, one dimensional histograms are plotted to check for irregularities. The one dimensional histograms for each training field are compared with the one dimensional histogram over the entire class of the training field. This produces many histograms, but is worth the effort to eliminate poor or mixed-class training fields, find errors in their class assignments, and also to verify that the classes are numerically separable. For the same reason, the J-M distance is computed and, for classes that are too close, the effects of an additional band or new training data are considered. As a result of these evaluations, some fields are redefined or rejected. Additional ground information may be necessary. Following this, an initial Bayesian classification is run, classifying only the areas defined by the training fields. Well separated classes produce training fields whose pixels are essentially all classified into the class of the field. These are checked and the training fields redefined and corrected. With this new training data, the full Bayesian classification is run on the complete area of interest. After the run, spatial information is used to modify the results. For example, the computed likelihoods are used to locally update the a priori values for a second classification as described in the previous section. The output is two new bands, the class band and the likelihood band. These are displayed so that a likelihood threshold for each class is selected by comparing various thresholds with the training data, knowledge of the area, and so on. Pixels whose likelihood is below the threshold are moved to the unclassified category, and the thresholded output is the final result.

If a good set of training data is used, and a sequence of steps such as this is followed, good classification results can be expected.

7.5   Problems in Classification

Problems areas in image classification are:

1. A priori inputs for Bayesian classifiers. Theoretically, if a certain class is known to occur in 1% of an image, the a priori probability for this class should be 1%. However, in practice, using such a low value will generally eliminate the class completely. Equal a priori values favor the infrequent classes, and the result is that selecting the proper values seems to be a mix of art and science.
2. Training data. Some studies suggest that the major factor affecting classification accuracy is not the classification method but the quality of the training data. The data for a class should not include other classes, yet must include a representative spread of pixels from the class. Getting a good set of training data is an important but difficult task.
3. Variability of data. Almost all types of data have a natural variability. For agricultural data, topography, view angle, sun angle, crop planting direction, water content, health, and age all induce a variability that cause class distributions to mix or be bi- or multi-modal. Checks of the class distributions such as one dimensional histograms help identify the problem. Solutions include splitting the classes, and using spatial information in the classifier.
4. Mixed pixels. The classification methods described assign each pixel to one class, implicitly assuming that whatever is contained within the pixel is all of that class. In reality, different classes may be mixed in a given pixel. In satellite data, this may occur in two ways: border pixels that cover portions of two adjacent ground cover types, such as neighboring wheat and corn fields;

and pixels of sparsely vegetated areas in which the vegetation and underlying soil is visible. The latter case occurs over rangelands and deserts, and early in the growing season for most crops. Border pixels in the training data cause an incorrect spreading in the class distribution. These can normally be avoided by selecting the training sets in the interior of fields. Incorrect classifications of border pixels may be reduced using spatial information. No standard methods exist to resolve the second mixed pixel problem.

7.6 Discussion

Accurate classification of remote sensing data is a lengthy process that requires working with field data and maps, as well as much interaction with a computer image processing system to enter data, plot histograms, check distributions, and so on. In addition, both preprocessing and postprocessing steps may be necessary. With these operations carefully applied and with good quality training data, classifications correctly identifying 85 to 95% of the pixels in a scene are often obtained.

7.7 Questions and Problems

1. Why are the a priori probabilities not included in the formula for J-M distance?
2. What is the difference between a minimum Mahalanobis distance classifier and the parametric Bayesian maximum likelihood classifier?
3. Show that the minimum Euclidean distance classifier is equivalent to a parametric Bayesian classifier for independent bands of equal variance with equal a priori probability values.
4. A minimum Euclidean distance classsfication is performed using four bands of data. Then the four principal components are computed and the same classification is performed on them. How do the results of the two classifications compare? Suppose

that a minimum city block distance classifier were used in both cases. How would the results compare?

5. A classification is to be done using a Gaussian parametric classifier. For one of the classes, the training data happens to be uniform, with all pixels equal to the same value. Referring to equation (7.1), can you see any problems that will result? Propose a solution.

8.0   Mathematical Background

8.1   Convolution and Correlation

A standard integral form, called a convolution integral, arises in many areas of analysis including image processing. The integral is of the form:

$$\int f(t)h(x-t)dt$$

and is denoted by $f*h$. A similar integral arises when computing the correlation coefficient between two functions. This is given by

$$\int f(t)h(t)dt$$

Often it is desired to find the point to which the function h must be shifted to give the best correlation with f. This is given by the value of x which maximizes:

$$\int f(t)h(t-x)dt$$

which is similar to the convolution integral, but with h reflected. If h is symmetric, $h(x) = h(-x)$ and the operations are identical.

In the digital case, the integrals become summations:

$$\sum_i f(i)h(m-i) \qquad \text{and} \qquad \sum_i f(i)h(i-m)$$

for convolution and correlation respectively, and there is one convolution/correlation value for each value of m. Image processing normally uses the two dimensional representations:

$$\sum_i \sum_j f(i,\ j)h(m-i, n-j) \qquad \text{and} \qquad \sum_i \sum_j f(i,\ j)h(i-m,\ j-n)$$

For most cases we consider of convolving a function h with f, h is symmetric (or anti-symmetric) and because of the nature of the calculation, we can ignore the reflection of h in the integral or summation. Thus convolution and correlation appear to be identical. However, as used in this book, there are two differences. First, when we speak of convolution, we are interested in the complete output function (or image) given by:

$$g(m,n) = \sum_i \sum_j f(i,\ j)h(m-i, n-j) = \sum_i \sum_j f(i,\ j)h(i-m,\ j-n)$$

(the second equality holds only for symmetric h). When we speak of correlation we are usually interested in the values of m and n giving the maximum of the summation. Secondly, when computing convolutions, we take the values as computed directly by the summation above, but for correlations, we typically normalize f and h so that the results are in the range $(-1, +1)$.

8.2   Principal Components

Many image processing operations work on several or all bands of an image. If there are many bands, it becomes difficult to visualize as well as expensive to process all the bands. The method of principal components allows us, in many cases, to reduce the dimensionality of our data; that is, to collapse the multiband image down to fewer bands.

Each pixel in an n band image may be considered as a point in n dimensional pixel space. The set of all pixels in the image becomes a distribution of points in this space. The axes of pixel space correspond one-to-one to the bands and, for $n = 3$, a pixel with value v_1 in band 1, v_2 in band 2, and v_3 in band 3 is expressed as the point (v_1, v_2, v_3). The effect of computing the principal components of a dis-

tribution is to determine a new set of axes with two related properties:

1. The axes may be ordered by their "information content". Thus
   using only the first axis, the best one dimensional representation
   of the data is obtained, by using the first two, the best two dimensional representation is obtained, and so on.
2. The data expressed in the new axes are uncorrelated.

For an image with m bands and n total pixels (n is the number of
lines times the number of samples) the transformation to principal
components is given by the equation:

$$Y = XE$$

where Y is the $n \times m$ matrix of data in the new basis, X the $n \times m$ matrix of data in the original basis, and E the $m \times m$ matrix whose columns are the eigenvectors of $X^T X$. In the image matrices X and Y,
the bands are arranged in one dimensional column vectors so that,
for example, the first column of X is the first original band, expressed as a one dimensional array. By convention, we arrange E so
that the eigenvector with the largest eigenvalue is first, the eigenvector with the next largest is second, and so on. Then the first column
of Y is the first principal component, the second column is the second principal component, etc.

An example of a four band input image and its four computed
principal components is shown in Figure 87 and Figure 88. The original four bands are from the LANDSAT MSS. Notice the lack of
information in the last two principal components.

8.3 Questions and Problems

1. Derive the principal component representation in two dimensions using the first property above.
   Let $v_1(i, j)$ and $v_2(i, j)$ for $i = 1, 2, \ldots, n_l$ and $j = 1, 2, \ldots, n_s$ be
   two bands of an image. n_l is the number of lines and n_s the number of samples per line so there are $n = n_l \times n_s$ total pixels. For

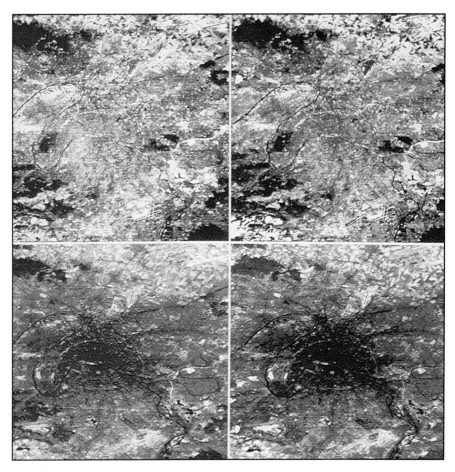

Figure 87. Original four image bands. Scene is LANDSAT 2 MSS of Paris, France.

simplicity of notation, reorder the bands into one dimensional arrays, and remove the mean from each band, to give

$$q_1(k) = v_1(i, j) - \bar{v}_1 \qquad \text{and} \qquad q_2(k) = v_2(i, j) - \bar{v}_2$$

where $k = (i - 1)n_s + j$, and $\bar{v}_1$ and $\bar{v}_2$ are the means in the two bands. k ranges from 1 to n. Also let

194

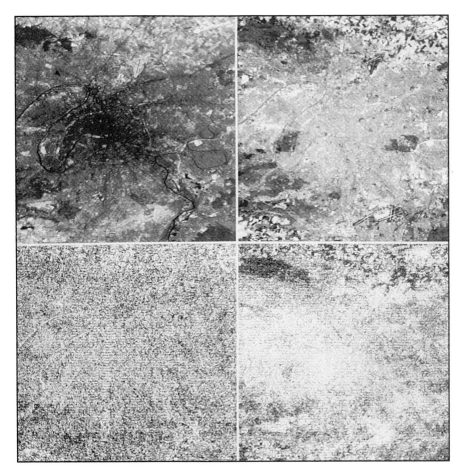

Figure 88. Computed principal component bands, in order, clockwise from top left.

$$\vec{x}_k = \begin{pmatrix} q_1(k) \\ q_2(k) \end{pmatrix}$$

Then $\vec{x}_k$ is the vector to $(q_1(k), q_2(k))$ in pixel space.

Find the new axes of pixel space by finding the unit vector $\vec{u}$ for which the off-axis components of the $\vec{x}_k$ are minimum (why?). That is, find $\vec{u}$ such that

$$f(\vec{u}) = \sum ||\vec{x}_k - (\vec{x}_k \cdot \vec{u})\vec{u}||$$

is minimum. To do this, take the derivative of $f(\vec{u})$ and set it to zero. For the derivative of the vector function, use the definition:

$$f(\vec{u}) = \lim_{||\Delta u|| \to 0} \frac{f(\vec{u} + \vec{\Delta u}) - f(\vec{u})}{||\vec{\Delta u}||}$$

where $\vec{u} = k\vec{v}$ for $\vec{v}$ perpendicular to $\vec{u}$ (why?), and find the value of $\vec{u}$ for which $f'(\vec{u})$ is zero.

2. Show that the principal components are uncorrelated. You can do this by showing that the covariance matrix C of the principal components may be written as Y^TY for Y as defined in Problem 1, and then simplify this expression.

9.0 Software Examples

This appendix contains code segments illustrating several of the functions described in the text. The examples are not complete programs for two reasons. First, complete programs would normally be longer, including error checking, reading of parameters, and so on. Secondly, image I/O functions are not listed. Most computer systems doing image processing have a standard set of routines to permit efficient read and write of image data. Such routines could be inserted at the commented places in the code below.

9.1 Histogram Matching in PL/I

The code segment below generates a pixel value mapping table from the histograms of an input image and a reference image. The table is constructed so that, if it were applied to the input image, its histogram would then match that of the reference image.

This code is taken from a program written using a variable naming convention in which the variable type is indicated by the first letter of the name. F indicates a full word integer (PL/I data type BIN FIXED(31)), H a half word integer (BIN FIXED(15)), and E a full word (single precision) floating point (BIN FLOAT(21)).

```
DCL                             /*                                              */
  F-REFHIST(0:255)  BIN FIXED(31),  /*THE REFERENCE HISTOGRAM               */
  F-REFPOP          BIN FIXED(31),  /*POPULATION OF REFERENCE IMAGE         */
  E-RSUM            BIN FLOAT(21),  /*REFERENCE CUMULATIVE PERCENT          */
  E-RPERCENT        BIN FLOAT(21),  /*REFERENCE ABSOLUTE PERCENT            */
  E-RCUM(0:255)     BIN FLOAT(21),  /*REFERENCE CUMULATIVE PERCENT          */
  F-INPHIST(0:255)  BIN FIXED(31),  /*THE INPUT HISTOGRAM                   */
  F-INPPOP          BIN FIXED(31),  /*POPULATION OF INPUT IMAGE             */
  E-ISUM            BIN FLOAT(21),  /*INPUT CUMULATIVE PERCENT              */
  E-IPERCENT        BIN FLOAT(21),  /*INPUT ABSOLUTE PERCENT                */
  E-ICUM(0:255)     BIN FLOAT(21),  /*INPUT CUMULATIVE PERCENT              */
  E-DIFF            BIN FLOAT(21),  /*DIFFERENCE FROM REF TO INPUT          */
  IRLAST            BIN FIXED(15),  /*LAST REF IMAGE VALUE MATCHED          */
  IRMIN             BIN FIXED(15),  /*INDEX OF MINIMUM DIFFERENCE           */
  K                 BIN FIXED(15),  /*LOOP INDEX                            */
  IX                BIN FIXED(15),  /*INDEX INTO TABLE CREATED              */
  E-MIN             BIN FLOAT(21),  /*MIN DIFF BETWEEN REF AND INP          */
  H-TABLE(0:255);   BIN FIXED(15);  /*TRANSLATE TABLE CONSTRUCTED           */
```

At start of code below, F-REFHIST contains the reference histogram, F-INPHIST contains the input histogram, and F-REFPOP and F-INPPOP the reference and input image populations. The output is H-TABLE, which is a pixel value mapping table so that element i translates input pixel value i. When applied to the image with histogram in F-INPHIST, that image will then have a histogram matching F-REFHIST.

```
Compute the cumulative histograms
E-RSUM=0.;
E-ISUM=0.;
DO I=0 TO 255;
  E-RPERCENT=F-REFHIST(I)/FLOAT(F-REFPOP);
  E-RSUM=E-RSUM+E-RPERCENT;
  E-RCUM(I)=E-RSUM;
  E-IPERCENT=F-INPHIST(I)/FLOAT(F-INPPOP);
  E-ISUM=E-ISUM+E-IPERCENT;
  E-ICUM(I)=E-ISUM;
END;
Now construct the table by finding the index into the reference cumulative histogram
giving the value closest to input cumulative histogram value. To save a little work,
start from IRLAST each time, the last value found.
IRLAST=0;
DO IX=0 TO 255;
  E-MIN=2.0;                              /*LARGER THAN LARGEST POSSIBLE */
  DO K=IRLAST TO 255;
  E-DIFF=ABS(E-ICUM(IX)-E-RCUM(K));
  IF E-DIFF < E-MIN THEN DO;
                    IRMIN=K;
                    E-MIN=E-DIFF;
  END;
  END;
  IRLAST=IRMIN;
  H-TABLE(IX)=IRMIN;
END
```

9.2 Window Processing in FORTRAN

Moving window operations are common in image processing. Many of the filters of chapter "Filtering" on page 69, for example, can be implemented as moving window operations. The code below performs a moving window operation, creating a new image in which the value of pixel at (i,j) is the standard deviation of the pixel values in a window centered at (i,j) in the input image.

SDW, the main routine, calls three subroutines SDWCL1, SDWLIN, and SDWUPD. The input image is held in a "rolling buffer" of 16 lines. Both the input and output image buffers are halfword integers. One feature to notice in the program is the way that it passes lines to subroutines. In this way, the subroutines can address the pixels as elements of one dimensional arrays instead of as two dimensional arrays. One dimensional addressing is faster, and using this method, a program such as this one runs about 30 to 35 % faster.

```
        PROGRAM  SDW
C
C     FUNCTION:  CREATE AN IMAGE IN WHICH EACH PIXEL IS THE STANDARD
C                DEVIATION OF THE PIXELS IN A WINDOW AROUND THE
C                CORRESPONDING PIXEL IN THE INPUT IMAGE.
C
        INTEGER*4  IFRSTL,ILASTL,ILINE,II(16),
C                  ISMA(1024),ISMASQ(1024),
C                  ILADD,ILDROP,ILTEMP,IWIND,K
        INTEGER*2  HIN(16*1024),HOUT(1024)
C
C     This program creates an output image in which each
C     pixel is equal to the standard deviation within
C     a IWIND x IWIND window about the corresponding pixel in the
C     input image.  The computation is done incrementally, computing
C     the standard deviation for pixel (i,j) from the values computed
C     for pixel (i,j-1) by dropping off old pixels, and adding on
C     new pixels.  The important arrays are ISMA and ISMASQ, giving
C     the sum and sum of squares of pixels across a line.
C
C     Comments starting with CIO indicate CALLs to an I/O
C     package, which must be supplied.  In these routines, it is
C     assumed that image pixels are read into and written from
C     halfword (INTEGER*2) arrays.
C
C     At the start of the code below, INUMLN has the number of lines
C     to process, ILINSZ is the line size (pixels per line), and
C     IWIND has the square window size.
C
C     For this code, the maximum size of IWIND is 16, and the input
C     image line size must be less than or equal to 1024.
C
C     SET UP THE II ARRAY OF INDICES INTO THE INPUT BUFFER HIN
        DO 101 K=1,16
            II(K)=(K-1)*1024 + 1
    101 CONTINUE
C
C     Do the first lines as a special case.
C
CIO     CALL IO to read the first IWIND input lines into the first
CIO     IWIND columns of HIN.  Notice that lines of the image are
CIO     stored in columns of HIN.  This is because FORTRAN stores
CIO     arrays by columns.  Storing the lines as columns avoids
CIO     reordering the data for I/O.
C
C     Compute column sums of vertical length IWIND across a line.
C
        CALL SDWCL1(HIN,ISMA,ISMASQ,IWIND,ILINSZ)
```

```
C
C       Compute square window sums across a line from the column sums
C       in ISMA and ISMSQA, putting the results in the output buffer HOUT
C
        CALL SDWLIN(ISMA,ISMASQ,IWIND,ILINSZ,HOUT)
C
C       Write out the first line ICNTRL times so that output
C       image will align with the input image.
        ICNTRL=(IWIND+1)/2
        DO 201 K=1,ICNTRL
CIO         CALL IO to write an output line from HOUT
    201 CONTINUE
C
C       Loop on the rest of the lines to be done
C
        IFRSTL=ICNTRL+1
        ILASTL=INUMLN-(IWIND-1)/2
        DO 302 ILINE=IFRSTL,ILASTL
C
C          Scroll the line pointers.  ILDROP is the line to drop,
C          ILADD is the line to add.
           ILDROP=II(1)
           DO 301 J=1,IWIND
              II(J)=II(J+1)
    301     CONTINUE
           II(IWIND+1)=ILDROP
           ILADD=II(IWIND)
CIO        CALL IO to read the next input line into HIN(ILADD)
C          Compute the next output line
           CALL SDWUPD(ISMA,ISMASQ,HIN(ILADD),HIN(ILDROP),ILINSZ)
           CALL SDWLIN(ISMA,ISMASQ,IWIND,ILINSZ,HOUT)
CIO        CALL IO to write an output line from HOUT

    302 CONTINUE
        ILASTL=ILASTL+1
C
C       Write out the last line multiple times so that the output
C       image will match in size the input image.
        DO 401 I=ILASTL,INUMLN
CIO        write an output line from HOUT
    401 CONTINUE
                    .
                    .
                    .
```

```fortran
      SUBROUTINE  SDWCL1(HIBUF,ISMA,ISMASQ,IWIND,ILINSZ)
C
C     FUNCTION:    AT EACH SAMPLE ACROSS A LINE, COMPUTE THE SUM
C                  AND SUM OF SQUARES OF PIXEL VALUES IN A COLUMN
C                  OF SIZE IWIND.
C
      INTEGER*2    HIBUF(1)
      INTEGER*4    ISMA(1),ISMASQ(1),IWIND,ILINSZ
      INTEGER*4    IVAL,ISUM,ISUMSQ
      INTEGER*2    I,J,INDX
C
      DO 210 I=1,ILINSZ
         ISUM=0
         ISUMSQ=0
         DO 200 J=1,IWIND
C            INDX ADDRESSES THE J-TH PIXEL IN THE I-TH LINE OF HIBUF
             INDX=I+(J-1)*1024
             IVAL=HIBUF(INDX)
             ISUM=ISUM+IVAL
             ISUMSQ=ISUMSQ+IVAL*IVAL
  200    CONTINUE
         ISMA(I)  =ISUM
         ISMASQ(I)=ISUMSQ
  210 CONTINUE
      RETURN
      END
```

```
      SUBROUTINE  SDWLIN(ISMA,ISMASQ,IWIND,ILINSZ,HOBUF)
C
C     FUNCTION:    THIS IS A SUBROUTINE OF SDW.  IT COMPUTES THE
C                  STANDARD DEVIATION ACROSS A LINE USING THE INPUT
C                  ARRAYS ISMA AND ISMASQ OF SUMS AND SUMS OF
C                  SQUARES. NOTE THAT THE OUTPUT STANDARD
C                  DEVIATION IS MULTIPLIED BY 10.
C
C     ISMA is an array of sums of pixel values.  ISMA(i) is the
C         sum of the pixels in a vertical column of size IWIND centered
C         on pixel i.
C     ISMASQ is an array of sums of squares of pixel values,
C         corresponding to ISMA.
C     IWIND  is the square window size
C     ILINSZ is the line size
C     HOBUF  is the output buffer
C
C     INPUT PARAMETERS
      INTEGER*4    ISMA(1),ISMASQ(1),IWIND,ILINSZ
      INTEGER*2    HOBUF(1)
C     LOCAL VARIABLES
      INTEGER*4    ISUM,ISUMSQ
      INTEGER*2    ISTART,IEND,IADD,IDROP
      REAL*4       STD,RNUM
C
C     DO THE FIRST "HALF-WINDOW" AS A SPECIAL CASE TO GET STARTED
C
      RNUM=IWIND*IWIND
      ISUM=0
      ISUMSQ=0
      DO 100 I=1,IWIND
         ISUM  =ISUM+ISMA(I)
         ISUMSQ=ISUMSQ + ISMASQ(I)
  100 CONTINUE
      STD =ISUMSQ - ISUM*ISUM/RNUM
      IF (STD.LT.0.) THEN
         WRITE(6,999) STD
         STD=0.
      ELSE
         ISTD=10. * SQRT(STD/RNUM) + 0.5
      END IF
C
C     NOW DO THE REST
C
      ISTART=   1 + (IWIND-1)/2
      IEND  =ILINSZ - (IWIND-1)/2
      DO 101 I=1,ISTART
         HOBUF(I)=ISTD
  101 CONTINUE
```

```
C
      IDROP=1
      IADD =IWIND+1
      ISTART=ISTART+1
      DO 210 I=ISTART,IEND
          ISUM  =ISUM  -ISMA(IDROP)  +ISMA(IADD)
          ISUMSQ=ISUMSQ-ISMASQ(IDROP)+ISMASQ(IADD)
          STD =ISUMSQ - ISUM*ISUM/RNUM
          IF (STD.LT.0.) THEN
             WRITE(6,999) STD
             STD=0.
          ELSE
             ISTD=10. * SQRT(STD/RNUM) + 0.5
          END IF
          HOBUF(I)=ISTD
          IDROP=IDROP+1
          IADD=IADD+1
  210 CONTINUE
C
C     DO THE LAST "HALF-WINDOW"
C
      IEND=IEND+1
      DO 300 I=IEND,ILINSZ
          HOBUF(I)=HOBUF(IEND-1)
  300 CONTINUE
      RETURN
  999 FORMAT(' NEGATIVE STD.  STD=',F14.4)
      END
```

```
      SUBROUTINE  SDWUPD(ISMA,ISMASQ,HIADD,HIDROP,ILINSZ)
C
C     FUNCTION:   UPDATES THE ISMA AND ISMASQ ARRAYS OF SUMS AND
C                 SUMS OF SQUARES BY DROPPING OFF A PIXEL ON THE
C                 LEFT EDGE AND ADDING ON A NEW PIXEL ON THE RIGHT.
C
      INTEGER*4     ISMA(1),ISMASQ(1),ILINSZ
      INTEGER*2     HIADD(1),HIDROP(1)
      INTEGER*4     IADD,IDROP
C
      DO 200 I=1,ILINSZ
          IADD    =HIADD(I)
          IDROP   =HIDROP(I)
          ISMA(I) =ISMA(I) -IDROP     + IADD
          ISMASQ(I)=ISMASQ(I)-IDROP*IDROP + IADD*IADD
  200 CONTINUE
      RETURN
      END
```

9.3 IHS to RGB Transformation in Pascal

```
procedure ihsrgb(int,hue,sat,r,g,b : real);
PURPOSE :  Convert from ihs to rgb.  Adapted from a program by
Allan F. Petersen and Ole Tidemann.

  const
      pi=3.14159265358;
  var
      sd1,sd2,sd3,stop,sbot,sglobalmax,slocalmax,imaxsat : real;
      m : array (.1..3,1..3.) of real;

  begin
      m(.1,1.):= 1.0;
      m(.1,2.):=-0.351561;
      m(.1,3.):= 1.486587;
      m(.2,1.):= 1.0;
      m(.2,2.):=-0.351561;
      m(.2,3.):=-0.755857;
      m(.3,1.):= 1.0;
      m(.3,2.):= 2.844450;
      m(.3,3.):= 0.0;

      begin
          sd1:=m(.1,2.)*cos(2*pi*hue)+m(.1,3.)*sin(2*pi*hue);
          sd2:=m(.2,2.)*cos(2*pi*hue)+m(.2,3.)*sin(2*pi*hue);
          sd3:=m(.3,2.)*cos(2*pi*hue)+m(.3,3.)*sin(2*pi*hue);
          stop:=0;
          if sd1<stop then stop:=sd1;
          if sd2<stop then stop:=sd2;
          if sd3<stop then stop:=sd3;
          stop:= - stop;
          sbot:=0;
          if sd1>sbot then sbot:=sd1;
          if sd2>sbot then sbot:=sd2;
          if sd3>sbot then sbot:=sd3;
          sglobalmax:=1/(stop+sbot);
          imaxsat:=stop*sglobalmax;
          if int < imaxsat then
              slocalmax:=sglobalmax*int/imaxsat
          else
              slocalmax:=sglobalmax*(1-int)/(1-imaxsat);
          r:=int+sat*slocalmax*sd1;
          g:=int+sat*slocalmax*sd2;
          b:=int+sat*slocalmax*sd3;
      end;
  end;
```

9.4 RGB to IHS Transformation in PL/I

```
RGBIHS: PROC (R,G,B,I,H,S);

Transforms from RGB to IHS. The I and H values for the input R, G, and B are com-
puted. These I and H values, together with S=1, are converted to RGB, giving r',g',b'.
From r' and the input R, the final saturation is computed. From a program by Francis-
co Ramirez, IBM Scientific Center, Madrid.

DCL                                    /*Calling sequence                  */
   R           BIN FLOAT(21),          /*Red value in the range (0,1)      */
   G           BIN FLOAT(21),          /*Green value in the range (0,1)    */
   B           BIN FLOAT(21),          /*Blue  value in the range (0,1)    */
   I           BIN FLOAT(21),          /*Intensity in the range (0,1)      */
   H           BIN FLOAT(21),          /*Hue in the range (0,1)            */
   S           BIN FLOAT(21);          /*Saturation in the range (0,1)     */
DCL                                    /*Other program variables           */
   RT          BIN FLOAT(21),          /*Temporary red                     */
   GT          BIN FLOAT(21),          /*Temporary green                   */
   BT          BIN FLOAT(21),          /*Temporary blue                    */
   GAMMA(2) BIN FLOAT(21),             /*Temporary variable                */
   MR(3,3)    BIN FLOAT(21) INIT       /*Inverse of the chromaticity       */
       ( .3    , .59   , .11  ,        /*matrix                            */
        -.105465 , -.207424 , .312889 , /*                                 */
         .445942 , -.445942 , .0    ),  /*                                 */
   PI2         BIN FLOAT(21)           /*Two pi                            */
       INIT(6.2831924);

I = MR(1,1)*R + MR(1,2)*G +  MR(1,3)*B; /*Intensity                        */
I = MAX(0.,MIN(1.,I));                 /*Clamp to (0,1)                    */

GAMMA(1) = MR(2,1)*R + MR(2,2)*G + MR(2,3)*B;   /*Hue                      *
GAMMA(2) = MR(3,1)*R + MR(3,2)*G + MR(3,3)*B;
IF ABS(GAMMA(1)) < 0.000001 & ABS(GAMMA(2)) < 0.000001 THEN
   H = 0.5;                           /*Default color for zero sat         */
ELSE
   H = ATAN(GAMMA(2),GAMMA(1))/PI2;
IF H < 0 THEN
   H = H+1.;                          /*Move to positive                  */
H = MAX(0.,MIN(1.,H));                /*Clamp to (0,1)                    */

   Insert subroutine to convert from IHS to RGB. The algorithm
   is identical to the one coded in PASCAL in the previous example.
CALL IHSRGB(I,H,1.0,RT,GT,BT);        /*Saturation                        */
IF RT = I THEN
   S = 0.;
ELSE
   S = (R-I)/(RT-I);
S = MAX(0.,MIN(1.,S));                /*Clamp to (0,1)                    */
END RGBIHS;
```

10.0   Bibliography

General References

1. Kenneth R. Castleman, *Digital Image Processing*, Prentice-Hall, 1979.
2. Rafael C. Gonzalez and Paul Wintz, *Digital Image Processing*, Addison-Wesley, 1977.
3. William K. Pratt, *Digital Image Processing*, Wiley and Sons, 1978.
4. Azriel Rosenfeld and Avinash C. Kak, *Digital Picture Processing*, Academic Press, 1982.

Chapter 2

5. Werner Frei, "Image Enhancement by Histogram Hyperbolization", Computer Graphics and Image Processing, 6, 1977, pp. 286-294.
6. Antonio Santisteban, "The Perceptual Color Space of Digital Image Display Terminals", IBM Journal of Research and Development, Vol. 27, Number 2, March 1983, pp. 127-132.
7. Alvy Ray Smith, "Color Gamut Transform Pairs", Proceedings of the ACM SIGGRAPH Conference, Vol. 12, Number 3, 1978, pp. 12-19.
8. J. M. Soha and A. A. Schwartz, "Multispectral Histogram Normalization Contrast Enhancement", Proceedings of the 5th Canadian Symposium on Remote Sensing, August 1978, pp. 86-93.
9. Johji Tajima, "Uniform Color Scale Applications to Computer Graphics", Computer Vision, Graphics, and Image Processing, 21, 1983, pp. 305-325.
10. Gunter Wyszecki and W. S. Stiles, *Color Science*, Wiley and Sons, 1967.

11. Status Report of the Graphics Standards Planning Committee, "Computer Graphics", Vol. 13, Number 3, August 1979, Appendix B.

Chapter 3

12. Roland T. Chin and C.-L. Yeh, "Quantitative Evaluation of Some Edge Preserving Noise Smoothing Filters", Computer Vision, Graphics, and Image Processing, Number 23, 1983.
13. M. Cocklin, G. Kaye, I. Kerr, P. Lams, "Digital Enhancement of Pneumothraces", First IEEE Computer Society International Symposium on Medical Imaging and Image Interpretation, October, 1982.
14. Henry P. Kramer and Judith B. Bruckner, "Iterations of a Non-Linear Transformation for Enhancement of Digital Images", Pattern Recognition, 7, 1975, pp. 53-58.
15. Jong-Sen Lee, "Digital Image Smoothing and the Sigma Filter", Computer Vision, Graphics, and Image Processing, 24, 1983, pp. 255-269.
16. David Marr, *Vision*, W. H. Freeman and Co., San Francisco, 1982.
17. Makoto Nagao and Takashi Matsutama, "Edge Preserving Smoothing", Computer Graphics and Image Processing, 9, 1979, pp. 394-407.
18. K. A. Narayanan and Azriel Rosenfeld, "Image Smoothing by Local Use of Global Information", IEEE Transactions on Systems, Man, and Cybernetics, Vol. SMC-11, No. 12, Dec 1981, pp. 826-831.
19. Tamar Peli and David Malah, "A Study of Edge Detection Algorithms", Computer Graphics and Image Processing, 20, 1982, pp. 1-21.
20. Azriel Rosenfeld, "A Nonlinear Edge Detection Technique", Proceedings of the IEEE, 58, May 1970, pp. 814-816.
21. David C. C. Wang, Anthony H. Vagnucci, and C. C. Li, "Gradient Inverse Weighted Smoothing Scheme and the Evaluation

of its Performance", Computer Graphics and Image Processing, 15, 1981, pp. 167-181.

Chapter 4

22. E. Oran Brigham, *The Fast Fourier Transform*, Prentice-Hall, 1974.
23. Paul Anuta, "Spatial Registration of Multispectral and Multi-temporal Digital Imagery Using Fast Fourier Transform Techniques", IEEE Transactions on Geoscience Electronics, Vol. GE-8, No. 4, Oct 1970, pp. 353-368.

Chapter 5

24. Louis Asfar, "A Method for Contour Detection, Segmentation, and Classification of a Landsat Scene," Proceedings of the International Geoscience and Remote Sensing Symposium, Washington, D. C., June, 1981.
25. Ralph L. Hartley, Leslie J. Kitchen, Cheng-Ye Wang, Azriel Rosenfeld, "Segmentation of FLIR Images: A Comparative Study", IEEE Transactions on Systems, Man, and Cybernetics, Vol. SMC-12, No. 4, July/Aug 1982.
26. Ralf Kohler, "A Segmentation System Based on Thresholding", Computer Graphics and Image Processing, Vol. 15, 1981, pp. 319-338.

Chapter 6

27. Ralph Bernstein, *Digital Image Processing for Remote Sensing*, IEEE Press, 1978,
28. Mark Cain and Dal Ferneyhough, "Accuracy Determination", internal technical memorandum, IBM FSD, 1977.
29. Franklin A. Graybill, *An Introduction to Linear Statistical Models*, McGraw-Hill, 1961.
30. Robert A. Schowengerdt, *Techniques for Image Processing and Classification in Remote Sensing*, Academic Press, 1983.

31. S. S. Rifman and D. M. McKinnon, "Evaluation of Digital Correction Techniques for ERTS Images," TRW Corporation Final Report, TRW 20634-6003-TU-00, NASA Goddard Space Flight Center, Greenbelt Maryland, March 1974.

Chapter 7

32. G. Ball and D. Hall, "A Clustering Technique for Summarizing Multivariate Data", Behavioral Science, 12, 1967, pp. 153-155.
33. Richard O. Duda and Peter E. Hart, *Pattern Classification and Scene Analysis*, Wiley, New York, 1973.
34. J. A. Richards, D. A. Landgrebe and P. H. Swain, "Overcoming Accuracy Deterioration in Pixel Relaxation Labeling," IEEE Fifth International Conference on Pattern Recognition, December, 1980.
35. Robert A. Schowengerdt, *Techniques for Image Processing and Classification in Remote Sensing*, Academic Press, 1983.
36. Philip H. Swain and Shirley M. Davis, *Remote Sensing: The Quantitative Approach*, McGraw-Hill, 1978.
37. J. T. Tou and R. C. Gonzalez, *Pattern Recognition Principles*, Addison-Wesley, 1974.

11.0 Index